600
LOW-COST
ELECTRONIC CIRCUITS

600
LOW-COST
ELECTRONIC CIRCUITS

David M. Gauthier

TAB BOOKS Inc.
Blue Ridge Summit, PA

FIRST EDITION
FIRST PRINTING

Copyright © 1989 by **TAB BOOKS Inc.**
Printed in the United States of America

Library of Congress Cataloging-in-Publication Data

Gauthier, David M.
    600 low-cost electronic circuits / by David M. Gauthier.
      p. cm.
    ISBN 0-8306-9219-3   ISBN 0-8306-3219-0 (pbk.)
    1. Electronic circuits—Design and construction. ii. Title.
  II. Title: Six hundred low-cost electronic circuits.
  TK7867.G36 1989
621.381′5—dc20   89-36602
                                          CIP

TAB BOOKS Inc. offers software for sale. For information and a catalog, please contact TAB Software Department, Blue Ridge Summit, PA 17294-0850.

Questions regarding the content of this book should be addressed to:

    Reader Inquiry Branch
    TAB BOOKS Inc.
    Blue Ridge Summit, PA 17294-0214

Acquisions Editor: Roland S. Phelps
Book Editor and Designer: Lisa A. Doyle
Production: Katherine Brown

Contents

Acknowledgments

The material presented here is reprinted from copyrighted material © 1988 with permission from the following companies:

Analog Devices, Inc.
One Technology Way
Norwood, MA 02062

Linear Technology Corp.
1630 McCarthy Blvd.
Milpitas, CA 95035

Motorola, Inc.
P.O. Box 20912
Phoenix, AZ 85036

Raytheon Company
Semiconductor Division
350 Ellis St.
Mountain View, CA 94039

Harris Corp. (RCA)
Box 3200
Somerville, NJ 08876

Siliconix, Inc.
2201 Laurelwood Rd.
Santa Clara, CA 95054

Introduction

I have endeavored to find circuitry that is useful not only to the electronics hobbyist but to technicians and engineers as well. Most of the circuits presented can be constructed for less than $20; however variety and versatility were foremost in the quest.

I have tried to obtain the most current applications circuitry available from a representative cross-section of manufacturers. I hope this book proves to be as useful and broad-based as it seemed while putting it together.

The first chapter consists of a broad range of amplifier-based circuitry. Many are operational amplifiers, but there are several differential and instrumentation amplifier schematics as well. Chapter 2 is a random sampling of array circuitry, useful for display purposes. Chapter 3 will help the technician or hobbyist with a bent toward computer circuitry by introducing several reputable comparator schematics.

Chapter 4 has a healthy sampling of A/D and D/A converters in 8- and 10-bit as well as high-speed versions. The chapter also contains telephone, voice-data, and radio communication and video surface-mount packages that should prove useful to both the experimenter and the professional. Chapter 5 is a diverse collection of special-purpose circuits that are unique. For example, several new automative-oriented circuits are presented.

Chapter 6 contains an assortment of various waveform oscillator circuits. Chapter 7 holds a quality assortment of converter circuits and power regulation circuits that should delight anyone looking for a dependable voltage or current source. Chapter 8 should please those of you who picture yourself as circuit designers. High-speed, proprietary high-voltage switches and multiplexers allow quicker switching and power dissipation for various applications.

Finally, the circuits in Chapter 9 should prove useful as a cost-effective alternative to A/D conversion using voltage-to-frequency converters (VFCs). They offer increased performance and use fewer external components. The voltage references are functionally similar to ordinary three-terminal fixed voltage regulators, but unlike zener-type references, they do not require external components and buffering. They also offer better initial accuracy, improved line and load regulation, and better temperature drift characteristics.

How to Use This Book

Each of the nine chapters contains a broad category of circuit type. Some chapters contain further subdivisions. Within each chapter (or, separately, within each subdivision), the participating manufacturers are listed alphabetically. A circuit or group of circuits is identified by a parenthetical code that identifies its manufacturer. The codes are placed after the subdivision head (in which case all the circuits in that group are from the same manufacturer), after the IC name (more than one circuit based on the same IC are grouped together), or after the figure caption. The codes are:

(AD)	Analog Devices
(LT)	Linear Technology
(MO)	Motorola
(RAY)	Raytheon
(RCA)	Harris (RCA)
(SIL)	Siliconix

Specific names of circuits are in the index at the back of the book. Following that is a component index for locating circuits that use a specific IC.

1

Amplifiers

GENERAL-PURPOSE AMPLIFIERS

MC1590G *(MO)*

60 MHz POWER GAIN TEST CIRCUIT

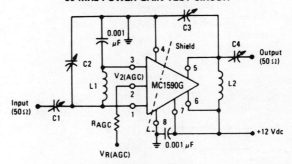

L1 = 7 Turns, #20 AWG Wire, 5/16″ Dia.,
5/8″ Long

L2 = 6 Turns, #14 AWG Wire, 9/16″ Dia.,
3/4″ Long

C1,C2,C3 = (1-30) pF
C4 = (1-10) pF

PROCEDURE FOR SETUP

Test	e_{in}	$V_2(AGC)$	$R_{AGC}(k\Omega)$
M_{AGC}	2.23 mV (−40dBm)	5-7 V	0
G_p	1.0 mV (−47dBm)	≤5.0 V	5.6
NF	1.0 mV (−47dBm)	≤5.0 V	5.6

VIDEO AMPLIFIER

3

30 MHz AMPLIFIER
(Power Gain = 50 dB, BW ≈ 1.0 MHz)

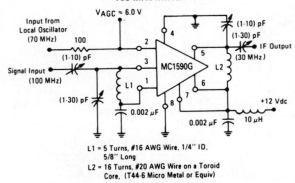

L1 = 12 Turns #22 AWG Wire on a Toroid Core,
(T37-6 Micro Metal or Equiv)
T1: Primary = 17 Turns #20 AWG Wire on a Toroid Core,
(T44-6 Micro Metal or Equiv)
Secondary = 2 Turns #20 AWG Wire

100 MHz MIXER

L1 = 5 Turns, #16 AWG Wire, 1/4" ID,
5/8" Long
L2 = 16 Turns, #20 AWG Wire on a Toroid
Core, (T44-6 Micro Metal or Equiv)

TWO-STAGE 60 MHz IF AMPLIFIER (Power Gain ≈ 80 dB, BW ≈ 1.5 MHz)

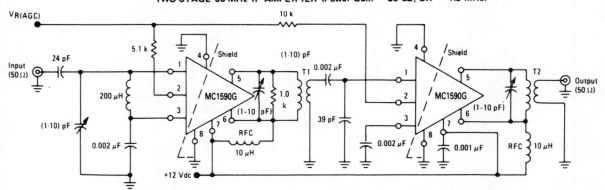

T1: Primary Winding = 15 Turns, #22 AWG Wire, 1/4" ID Air Core
Secondary Winding = 4 Turns #22 AWG Wire,
Coefficient of Coupling ≈ 1.0

T2: Primary Winding = 10 Turns, #22 AWG Wire, 1/4" ID Air Core
Secondary Winding = 2 Turns, #22 AWG Wire,
Coefficient of Coupling ≈ 1.0

12.5-WATT WIDEBAND POWER AMPLIFIER

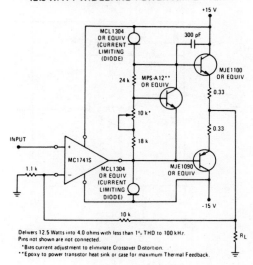

Delivers 12.5 Watts into 4.0 ohms with less than 1% THD to 100 kHz.
Pins not shown are not connected.

*Bias current adjustment to eliminate Crossover Distortion.
**Epoxy to power transistor heat sink or case for maximum Thermal Feedback.

MC1776,C *(MO)*

GATED AMPLIFIER

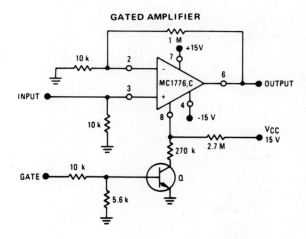

WIEN BRIDGE OSCILLATOR

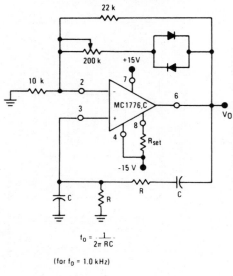

$$f_0 = \frac{1}{2\pi\,RC}$$

(for f_0 = 1.0 kHz)

R = 16 kΩ
C = 0.01 μF

MULTIPLE FEEDBACK BANDPASS FILTER

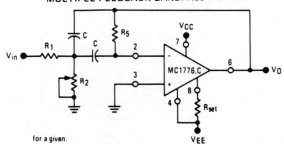

for a given:
  f_0 = center frequency
  $A\,(f_0)$ = Gain at center frequency
  Q = quality factor
Choose a value for C, then

$$R_5 = \frac{Q}{\pi f_0 C}$$

$$R1 = \frac{R5}{2A\,(f_0)}$$

$$R2 = \frac{R1 \cdot R5}{4Q^2\,R1 - R5}$$

To obtain less than 10% error from the operational amplifier:

$$\frac{Q_0\,f_0}{GBW} < 0.1$$

where f_0 and GBW are expressed in Hz. GBW is available from Figure 6 as a function of Set Current, I_{set}.

MULTIPLE FEEDBACK BANDPASS FILTER

(1.0 kHz)

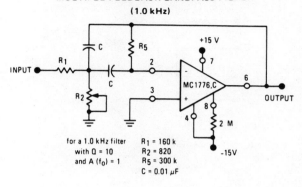

for a 1.0 kHz filter
with Q = 10
and A (f_o) = 1

R_1 = 160 k
R_2 = 820
R_5 = 300 k
C = 0.01 μF

HIGH INPUT IMPEDANCE AMPLIFIER

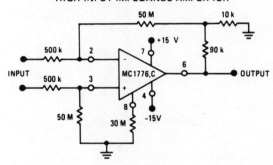

LM101A, LM201A, LM301A *(MO)*

LOGIC "NAND" GATE (Large Fan-In)

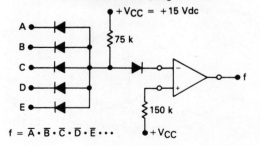

$f = \overline{A} \cdot \overline{B} \cdot \overline{C} \cdot \overline{D} \cdot \overline{E} \cdots$

7

LOGIC "NOR" GATE

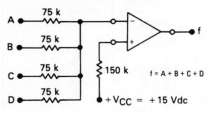

$$f = A + B + C + D$$

$$f = \overline{A} + \overline{B} + \overline{C} + \overline{D}$$

R-S FLIP-FLOP

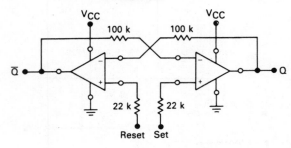

ASTABLE MULTIVIBRATOR

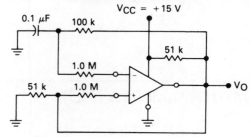

POSITIVE-EDGE DIFFERENTIATOR

Output Rise Time ≈ 0.22 ms
Input Change Time Constant ≈ 1.0 ms

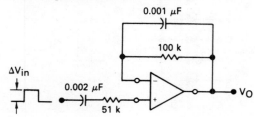

NEGATIVE-EDGE DIFFERENTIATOR

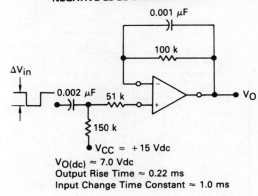

$V_{O(dc)} \approx 7.0$ Vdc
Output Rise Time ≈ 0.22 ms
Input Change Time Constant ≈ 1.0 ms

MC3301, MC3401, LM2900, LM3900 *(MO)*

INVERTING AMPLIFIER

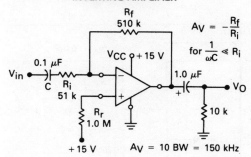

$$A_V = -\frac{R_f}{R_i}$$

for $\frac{1}{\omega C} \ll R_i$

$A_V = 10$ BW $= 150$ kHz

NONINVERTING AMPLIFIER

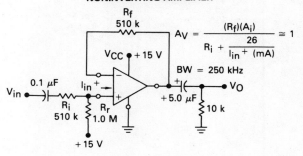

$$A_V = \frac{(R_f)(A_i)}{R_i + \dfrac{26}{I_{in}^+ \text{ (mA)}}} \cong 1$$

BW $= 250$ kHz

9

BASIC BANDPASS AND NOTCH FILTER

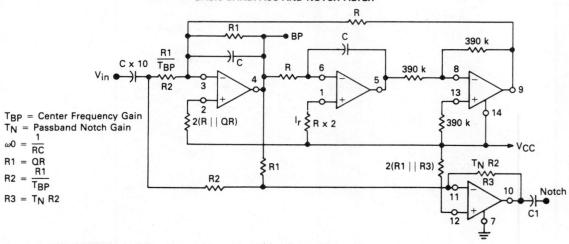

T_{BP} = Center Frequency Gain
T_N = Passband Notch Gain
$\omega 0 = \dfrac{1}{RC}$
$R1 = QR$
$R2 = \dfrac{R1}{T_{BP}}$
$R3 = T_N R2$

BANDPASS AND NOTCH FILTER

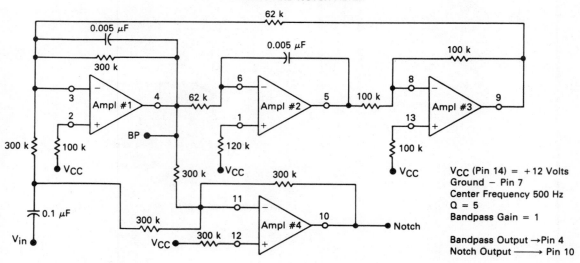

V_{CC} (Pin 14) = +12 Volts
Ground − Pin 7
Center Frequency 500 Hz
Q = 5
Bandpass Gain = 1

Bandpass Output →Pin 4
Notch Output ———→ Pin 10

10

INVERTING AMPLIFIER WITH ARBITRARY REFERENCE

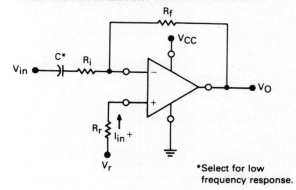

*Select for low frequency response.

INVERTING AMPLIFIER WITH A_v = 100 AND V_r = V_{CC}

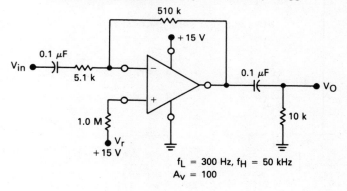

f_L = 300 Hz, f_H = 50 kHz
A_v = 100

AMPLIFIER AND DRIVER FOR A 50-OHM LINE

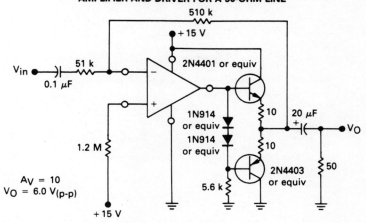

A_V = 10
V_O = 6.0 $V_{(p\text{-}p)}$

MC3403 *(MO)*

FUNCTION GENERATOR

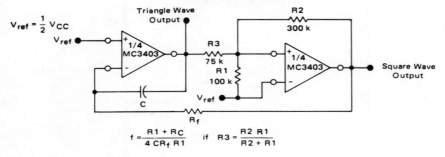

$$f = \frac{R1 + RC}{4\,CR_f\,R1} \quad \text{if} \quad R3 = \frac{R2\,R1}{R2 + R1}$$

MULTIPLE FEEDBACK BANDPASS FILTER

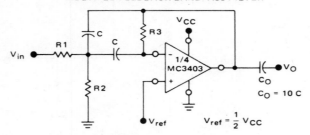

$C_O = 10\,C$

$V_{ref} = \frac{1}{2}\,V_{CC}$

Given f_o = Center Frequency

         $A(f_o)$ = Gain at Center Frequency

Choose Value f_o, C

     Then:

$$R3 = \frac{Q}{\pi\,f_o\,C}$$

$$R1 = \frac{R3}{2\,A(f_o)}$$

$$R2 = \frac{R1\,R5}{4Q^2\,R1 - R5}$$

For less than 10% error from operational amplifier

$$\frac{Q_o\,f_o}{BW} < 0.1 \qquad \text{Where } f_o \text{ and BW are expressed in Hz.}$$

If source impedance varies, filter may be preceded with voltage follower buffer to stabilize filter parameters.

MC3405, MC3505 *(MO)*

HIGH/LOW LIMIT ALARM

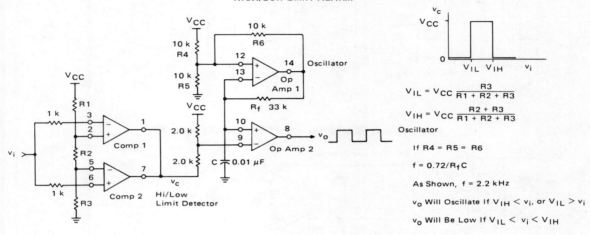

$$V_{IL} = V_{CC} \frac{R3}{R1 + R2 + R3}$$

$$V_{IH} = V_{CC} \frac{R2 + R3}{R1 + R2 + R3}$$

Oscillator

If R4 = R5 = R6

$f = 0.72/R_f C$

As Shown, $f = 2.2\,kHz$

v_o Will Oscillate If $V_{IH} < v_i$, or $V_{IL} > v_i$

v_o Will Be Low If $V_{IL} < v_i < V_{IH}$

SQUELCH CIRCUIT FOR AM OR FM

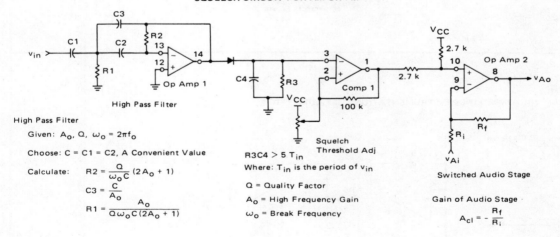

High Pass Filter

Given: A_o, Q, $\omega_o = 2\pi f_o$

Choose: C = C1 = C2, A Convenient Value

Calculate: $R2 = \dfrac{Q}{\omega_o C}(2A_o + 1)$

$C3 = \dfrac{C}{A_o}$

$R1 = \dfrac{A_o}{Q \omega_o C (2A_o + 1)}$

$R3C4 > 5\,T_{in}$

Where: T_{in} is the period of v_{in}

Q = Quality Factor

A_o = High Frequency Gain

ω_o = Break Frequency

Switched Audio Stage

Gain of Audio Stage

$$A_{cl} = - \frac{R_f}{R_i}$$

13

WINDOW COMPARATOR

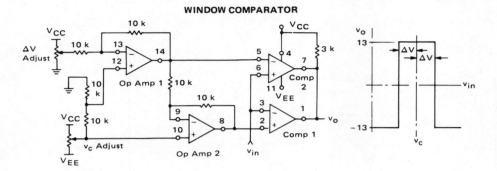

ZERO CROSSING DETECTOR WITH TEMPERATURE SENSOR

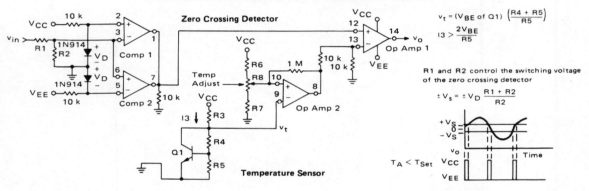

$$v_t = (V_{BE} \text{ of } Q1) \left(\frac{R4 + R5}{R5} \right)$$

$$I3 > \frac{2V_{BE}}{R5}$$

R1 and R2 control the switching voltage of the zero crossing detector

$$\pm V_s = \pm V_D \frac{R1 + R2}{R2}$$

HIGH IMPEDANCE INSTRUMENTATION BUFFER/FILTER (MO)

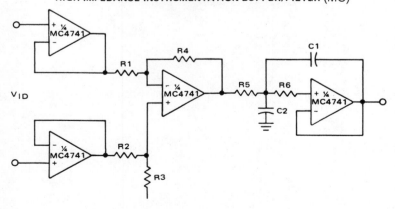

4-BIT PARALLEL A/D CONVERTER (MO)

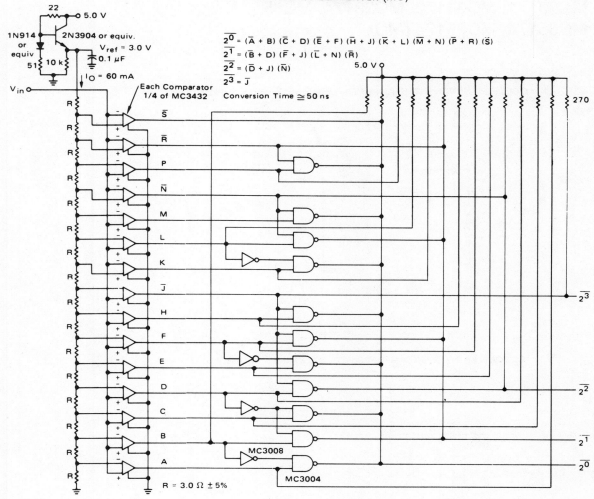

$$\overline{2^0} = (\overline{A} + B)\,(\overline{C} + D)\,(\overline{E} + F)\,(\overline{H} + J)\,(\overline{K} + L)\,(\overline{M} + N)\,(\overline{P} + R)\,(\overline{S})$$
$$\overline{2^1} = (\overline{B} + D)\,(\overline{F} + J)\,(\overline{L} + N)\,(\overline{R})$$
$$\overline{2^2} = (\overline{D} + J)\,(\overline{N})$$
$$\overline{2^3} = \overline{J}$$

Conversion Time $\cong$ 50 ns

Each Comparator 1/4 of MC3432

V_{ref} = 3.0 V

I_O = 60 mA

V_{in}

1N914 or equiv

2N3904 or equiv.

0.1 μF

5.0 V

22

51

10 k

270

R = 3.0 Ω ± 5%

MC3008

MC3004

MC33171, MC33172, MC33174, MC35171, MC35172, MC35174 *(MO)*

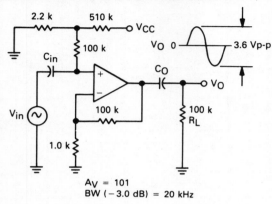

AC COUPLED NONINVERTING AMPLIFIER WITH SINGLE +5.0 V SUPPLY

$A_V = 101$
BW (−3.0 dB) = 20 kHz

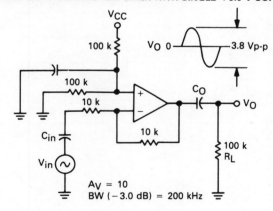

AC COUPLED INVERTING AMPLIFIER WITH SINGLE +5.0 V SUPPLY

$A_V = 10$
BW (−3.0 dB) = 200 kHz

DC COUPLED INVERTING AMPLIFIER
MAXIMUM OUTPUT SWING WITH SINGLE
+5.0 V SUPPLY

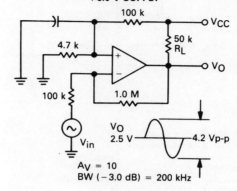

$A_V = 10$
$BW \ (-3.0 \ dB) = 200 \ kHz$

OFFSET NULLING CIRCUIT

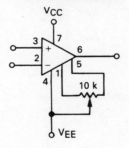

Offset Nulling range is approximately ±80 mV
with a 10 k potentiometer, MC33171/MC35171 only.

ACTIVE HIGH-Q NOTCH FILTER

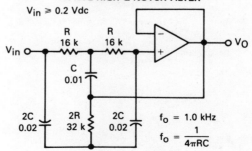

$f_o = 1.0 \ kHz$

$f_o = \dfrac{1}{4\pi RC}$

ACTIVE BANDPASS FILTER

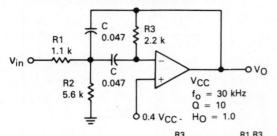

Given f_O = Center Frequency
A_O = Gain at Center Frequency
Choose Value f_O, Q, A_O, C
Then
For less than 10% error from operational amplifier
Where f_O and GBW are expressed in Hz.

$$R1 = \frac{R3}{2 H_O}$$

$$R2 = \frac{R1\,R3}{4Q^2\,R1 - R3}$$

$$R3 = \frac{Q}{\pi f_O C}$$

$$\frac{Q_O\,f_O}{GBW} < 0.1$$

MC34001, MC35001, MC34002, MC35002, MC34004, MC35004 *(MO)*

LONG INTERVAL RC TIMER

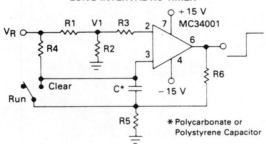

Time (t) = R4 C$\ln$ ($V_R/V_R - V_I$), $R_3 = R_4$, $R_5 = 0.1\,R_6$
If R1 = R2: t = 0.693 R4C

Design Example: 100 Second Timer
V_R = 10 v   C = 1.0 μF   R3 = R4 = 144 M
R6 = 20 k   R5 = 2.0 k   R1 = R2 = 1.0 k

POSITIVE PEAK DETECTOR

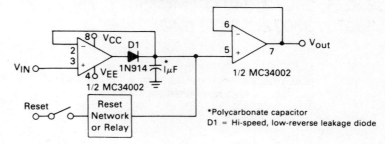

Reset

*Polycarbonate capacitor
D1 = Hi-speed, low-reverse leakage diode

ISOLATING LARGE CAPACITIVE LOADS

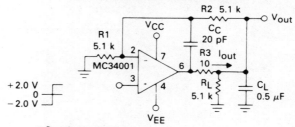

- Overshoot <10%
- t_s = 10 μs
- When driving large C_L, the V_{out} slew rate is determined by C_L and $I_{out(max)}$:

$$\frac{\Delta V_{out}}{\Delta t} = \frac{I_{out}}{C_L} = \frac{0.02}{0.5} \text{ V/μs} = 0.04 \text{ V/μs (with } C_L \text{ shown)}$$

WIDE BW, LOW NOISE, LOW DRIFT AMPLIFIER

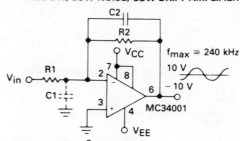

- Power BW: $f_{max} = \frac{S_r}{2\pi V_p} \cong 240$ kHz

- Parasitic input capacitance (C1 ≅ 3 pF plus any additional layout capacitance) interacts with feedback elements and creates undesirable high-frequency pole. To compensate add C2 such that: R2C2 ≅ R1C1.

19

MC34071, 34072, 34074 / MC35071, 35072, 35074 / MC33071, 33072, 33074 *(MO)*

TYPICAL SINGLE SUPPLY APPLICATIONS V$_{CC}$ = 5.0 VOLTS
AC COUPLED NONINVERTING AMPLIFIER

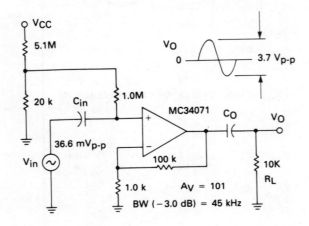

ACTIVE BANDPASS FILTER

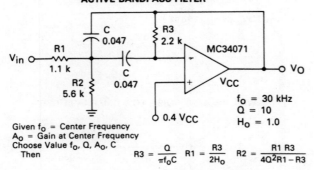

Given f$_O$ = Center Frequency
A$_O$ = Gain at Center Frequency
Choose Value f$_O$, Q, A$_O$, C
Then

$$R3 = \frac{Q}{\pi f_O C} \quad R1 = \frac{R3}{2H_O} \quad R2 = \frac{R1\,R3}{4Q^2 R1 - R3}$$

For less than 10% error from operational amplifier

$$\frac{Q_O f_O}{GBW} < 0.1$$

Where f$_O$ and GBW are expressed in Hz.
GBW = 4.5 MHz Typ.

AC COUPLED INVERTING AMPLIFIER

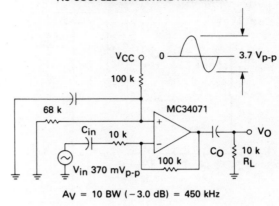

$$A_V = 10 \; BW \; (-3.0 \; dB) = 450 \; kHz$$

DC COUPLED INVERTING AMPLIFIER MAXIMUM OUTPUT SWING

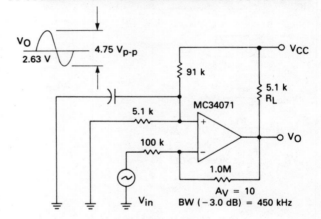

$$A_V = 10$$
$$BW \; (-3.0 \; dB) = 450 \; kHz$$

UNITY GAIN BUFFER TTL DRIVER

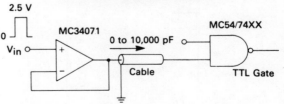

ACTIVE HIGH-Q NOTCH FILTER

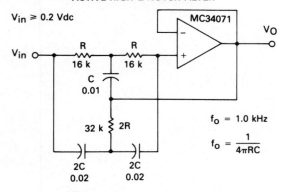

$V_{in} \geq 0.2$ Vdc

V_{in}

R 16 k   R 16 k   MC34071 V_O

C 0.01

32 k   2R

2C 0.02   2C 0.02

$f_O = 1.0$ kHz

$f_O = \dfrac{1}{4\pi RC}$

LOW INPUT VOLTAGE COMPARATOR WITH HYSTERESIS

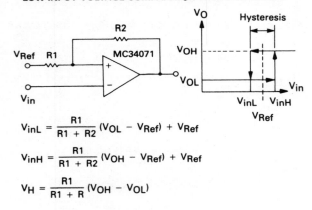

R2   MC34071

V_{Ref} R1

V_{in}

V_O Hysteresis

V_{OH}

V_{OL}

V_{in}

V_{inL} V_{inH}

V_{Ref}

$$V_{inL} = \frac{R1}{R1 + R2}(V_{OL} - V_{Ref}) + V_{Ref}$$

$$V_{inH} = \frac{R1}{R1 + R2}(V_{OH} - V_{Ref}) + V_{Ref}$$

$$V_H = \frac{R1}{R1 + R}(V_{OH} - V_{OL})$$

HIGH COMPLIANCE VOLTAGE TO SINK CURRENT CONVERTER

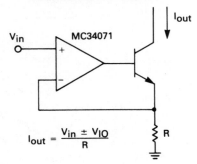

V_{in} MC34071 I_{out}

$$I_{out} = \frac{V_{in} \pm V_{IO}}{R}$$

R

HIGH INPUT IMPEDANCE DIFFERENTIAL AMPLIFIER

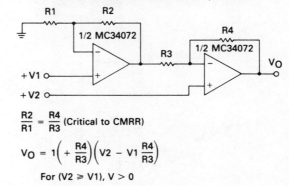

$$\frac{R2}{R1} = \frac{R4}{R3} \text{ (Critical to CMRR)}$$

$$V_O = 1\left(+\frac{R4}{R3}\right)\left(V2 - V1\frac{R4}{R3}\right)$$

For (V2 ≥ V1), V > 0

BRIDGE CURRENT AMPLIFIER

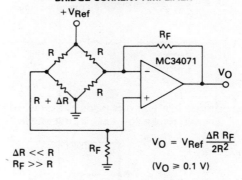

$\Delta R << R$
$R_F >> R$

$$V_O = V_{Ref}\frac{\Delta R\ R_F}{2R^2}$$

$(V_O \geq 0.1\ V)$

LOW VOLTAGE PEAK DETECTOR

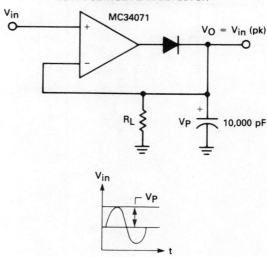

HIGH FREQUENCY PULSE WIDTH MODULATION

$$f_{OSC} \cong \frac{0.85}{RC}$$

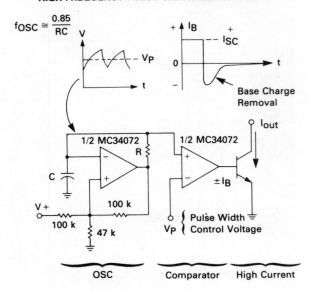

OSC   Comparator   High Current

GENERAL ADDITIONAL APPLICATIONS INFORMATION V_S = ±15 VOLTS
SECOND ORDER LOW-PASS ACTIVE FILTER

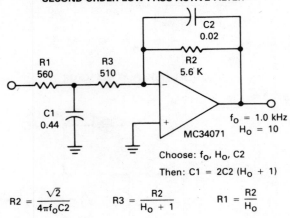

f_O = 1.0 kHz
H_O = 10

Choose: f_O, H_O, C2

Then: C1 = 2C2 (H_O + 1)

$$R2 = \frac{\sqrt{2}}{4\pi f_O C2} \qquad R3 = \frac{R2}{H_O + 1} \qquad R1 = \frac{R2}{H_O}$$

SECOND ORDER HIGH-PASS ACTIVE FILTER

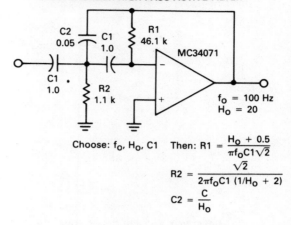

Choose: f_O, H_O, C1   Then: $R1 = \dfrac{H_O + 0.5}{\pi f_O C1 \sqrt{2}}$

$$R2 = \dfrac{\sqrt{2}}{2\pi f_O C1\ (1/H_O + 2)}$$

$$C2 = \dfrac{C}{H_O}$$

FAST SETTLING INVERTER

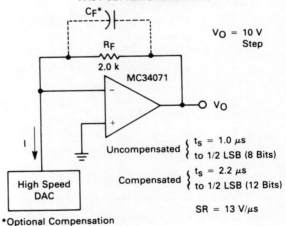

$V_O = 10\ V$
Step

Uncompensated $\begin{cases} t_S = 1.0\ \mu s \\ \text{to } 1/2\ \text{LSB (8 Bits)} \end{cases}$

Compensated $\begin{cases} t_S = 2.2\ \mu s \\ \text{to } 1/2\ \text{LSB (12 Bits)} \end{cases}$

$SR = 13\ V/\mu s$

*Optional Compensation

UNITY GAIN BUFFER ($A_V = +1.0$)

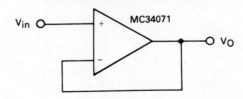

$BW_P = 200\ kHz$
$V_O = 20\ V_{p\text{-}p}$
$SR = 10\ V/\mu s$

BASIC INVERTING AMPLIFIER

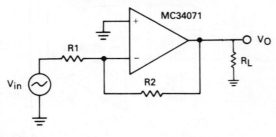

$$\frac{V_O}{V_{in}} = \frac{R2}{R1} \quad \text{BW} \; (-3.0 \; \text{dB} = \text{GBW} \left[\frac{R1}{R1 + R2} \right]$$

$$\text{SR} = 13 \; \text{V}/\mu\text{s}$$

BASIC NON INVERTING AMPLIFIER

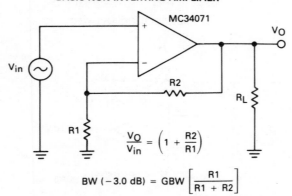

$$\frac{V_O}{V_{in}} = \left(1 + \frac{R2}{R1} \right)$$

$$\text{BW} \; (-3.0 \; \text{dB}) = \text{GBW} \left[\frac{R1}{R1 + R2} \right]$$

NE592, SE592 *(MO)*

DIFFERENTIAL AMPLIFIER
FILTER NETWORKS

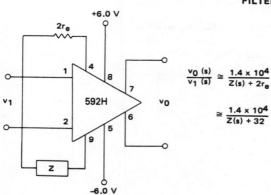

$$\frac{v_0 \; (s)}{v_1 \; (s)} \cong \frac{1.4 \times 10^4}{Z(s) + 2r_e}$$

$$\cong \frac{1.4 \times 10^4}{Z(s) + 32}$$

BASIC CONFIGURATION

Z NETWORK	FILTER TYPE	v_0 (s) TRANSFER v_1 (s) FUNCTION
R L	Low Pass	$\frac{1.4 \times 10^4}{L} \left[\frac{1}{s + R/L} \right]$
R C	High Pass	$\frac{1.4 \times 10^4}{R} \left[\frac{s}{s + 1/RC} \right]$
R L C	Band Pass	$\frac{1.4 \times 10^4}{L} \left[\frac{s}{s^2 + R/L \, s + 1/LC} \right]$
R L C	Band Reject	$\frac{1.4 \times 10^4}{R} \left[\frac{s^2 + 1/LC}{s^2 + 1/LC + s/RC} \right]$

NOTE:
In the networks above, the R value used is assumed
to include 2 r_e, or approximately 30 Ohms.

DISK/TAPE PHASE MODULATED READBACK SYSTEMS

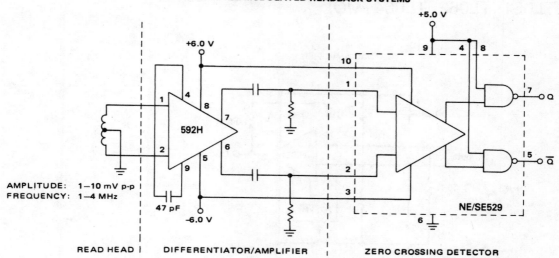

AMPLITUDE: 1–10 mV p-p
FREQUENCY: 1–4 MHz

READ HEAD | DIFFERENTIATOR/AMPLIFIER | ZERO CROSSING DETECTOR

DIFFERENTIATION WITH HIGH COMMON MODE NOISE REJECTION

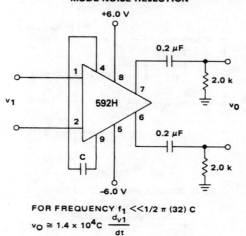

FOR FREQUENCY $f_1 \ll 1/2 \pi (32) C$

$$v_O \cong 1.4 \times 10^4 C \frac{d_{v1}}{dt}$$

27

TL061, TL062, TL064 *(MO)*

AC AMPLIFIER

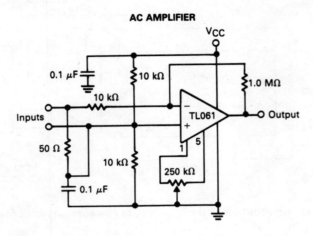

HIGH-Q NOTCH FILTER

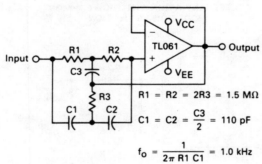

$$R1 = R2 = 2R3 = 1.5 \text{ M}\Omega$$

$$C1 = C2 = \frac{C3}{2} = 110 \text{ pF}$$

$$f_o = \frac{1}{2\pi \, R1 \, C1} = 1.0 \text{ kHz}$$

0.5 Hz SQUARE-WAVE OSCILLATOR

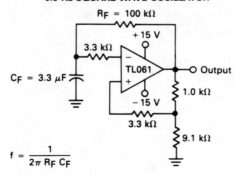

$$f = \frac{1}{2\pi \, R_F \, C_F}$$

INSTRUMENTATION AMPLIFIER

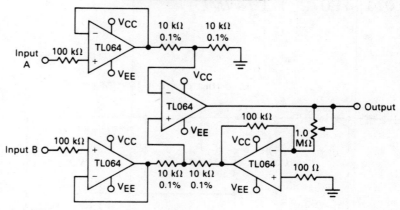

AUDIO DISTRIBUTION AMPLIFIER

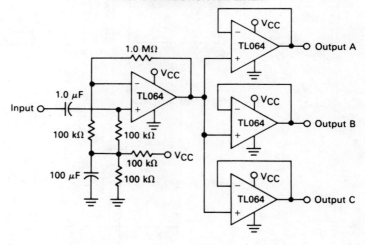

TL071, TL072, TL074 *(MO)*

AUDIO TONE CONTROL AMPLIFIER

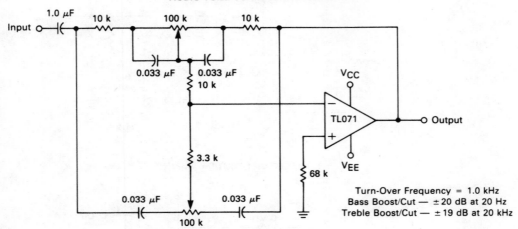

Turn-Over Frequency = 1.0 kHz
Bass Boost/Cut — ±20 dB at 20 Hz
Treble Boost/Cut — ±19 dB at 20 kHz

HIGH Q NOTCH FILTER

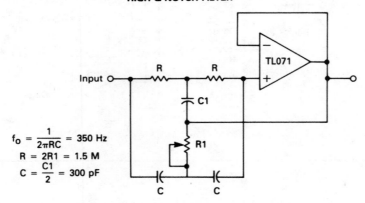

$$f_O = \frac{1}{2\pi RC} = 350 \text{ Hz}$$
$$R = 2R1 = 1.5 \text{ M}$$
$$C = \frac{C1}{2} = 300 \text{ pF}$$

TL081, TL082, TL084 *(MO)*

POSITIVE PEAK DETECTOR

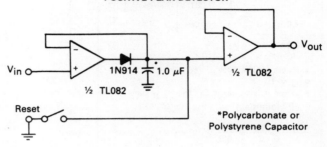

LONG INTERVAL RC TIMER

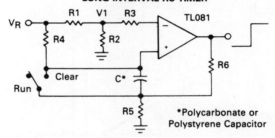

Time (t) = R4 Cℓn (V$_R$/V$_R$ − V$_1$), R$_3$ = R$_4$, R$_5$ = 0.1 R6
 If R1 = R2: t = 0.693 R4C
Design Example: 100 Second Timer

V$_R$ = 10 V	C = 1.0 μF	R3 = R4 = 144 M
R6 = 20 k	R5 = 2.0 k	R1 = R2 = 1.0 k

VOLTAGE CONTROLLED CURRENT SOURCE

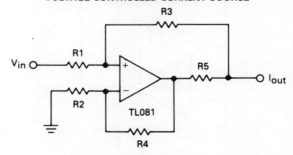

If R1 through R4 >> R5 then I$_{out}$ = $\dfrac{V_{in}}{R5}$

ISOLATING LARGE CAPACITIVE LOADS

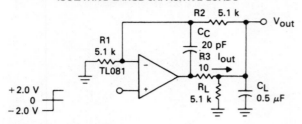

- Overshoot < 10%
- t_s = 10 μs
- When driving large C_L, the V_{out} slew rate is determined by C_L and $I_{out(max)}$:

$$\frac{\Delta V_{out}}{\Delta t} = \frac{I_{out}}{C_L} \cong \frac{0.02}{0.5} \text{ V/}\mu\text{s} = 0.04 \text{ V/}\mu\text{s (with } C_L \text{ shown)}$$

Si7652 *(SIL)*

Inverting Amplifier

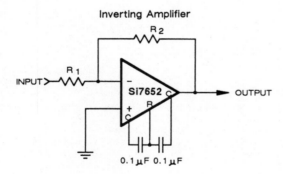

Non–inverting Amplifier

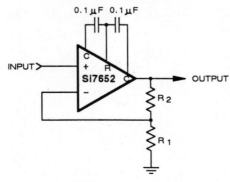

Using the 741 to Boost the Output
of the Si7652

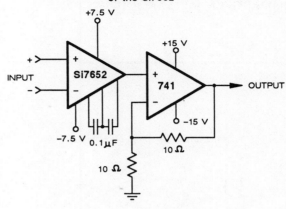

Nulling a High Speed Op-Amp

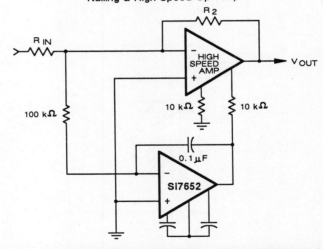

INSTRUMENTATION AMPLIFIERS

AD521 *(AD)*

Transformer Coupled, Direct Return

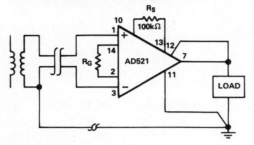

Thermocouple, Direct Return

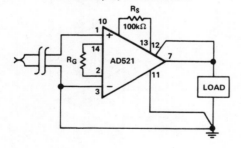

AC Coupled, Indirect Return
Ground Returns for "Floating" Transducers

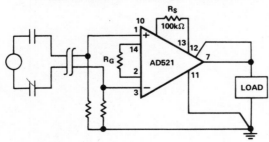

Operating Conditions for $V_{IN} \approx V_S = 10V$

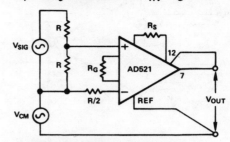

1. INCREASE R_G TO PICK UP GAIN LOST BY R DIVIDER NETWORK
2. INPUT SIGNAL MUST BE REDUCED IN PROPORTION TO POWER SUPPLY VOLTAGE LEVEL

AD524 (AD)

Operating Connections for G = 100

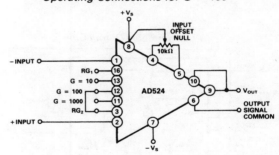

Gain of 2000

$$G = \frac{(R_2 \| 40k) + R_1 + R_2}{(R_2 \| 40k)}$$

$(R_1 + R_2 + R_3) \| R_L \geq 2k$

Operating Connections for G = 20, Low Gain T.C. Technique

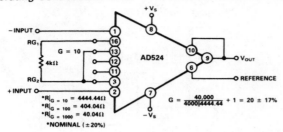

$$G = \frac{40,000}{4000 \| 4444.44} + 1 = 20 \pm 17\%$$

*$R|_{G\ =\ 10} = 4444.44\Omega$
*$R|_{G\ =\ 100} = 404.04\Omega$
*$R|_{G\ =\ 1000} = 40.04\Omega$
*NOMINAL (±20%)

Operating Connections for G = 20

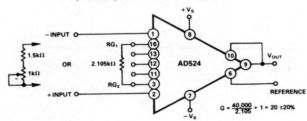

$$G = \frac{40,000}{2.105} + 1 = 20 \pm 20\%$$

Programmable Output Gain

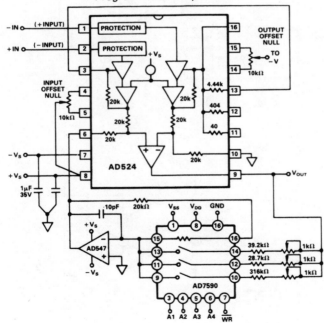

Programmable Output Gain Using a DAC

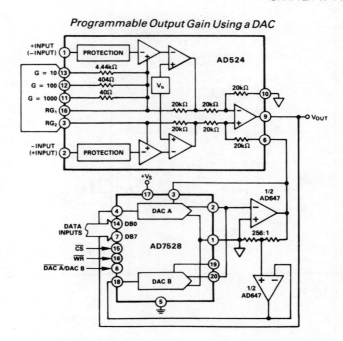

Auto-Zero Circuit

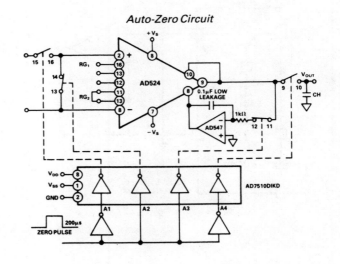

Software Controllable Offset

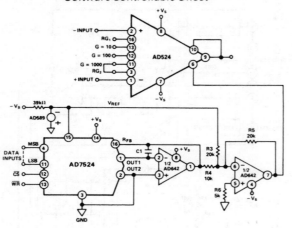

AD521 *(AD)*

± 5V Precision Instrumentation Amplifier (LT)

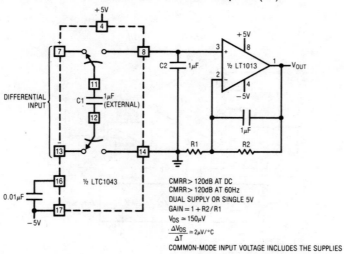

CMRR > 120dB AT DC
CMRR > 120dB AT 60Hz
DUAL SUPPLY OR SINGLE 5V
GAIN = 1 + R2/R1
$V_{OS} \approx 150\mu V$
$\frac{\Delta V_{OS}}{\Delta T} = 2\mu V/^{\circ}C$
COMMON-MODE INPUT VOLTAGE INCLUDES THE SUPPLIES

Chopper-Stabilized Instrumentation Amplifier (LT)

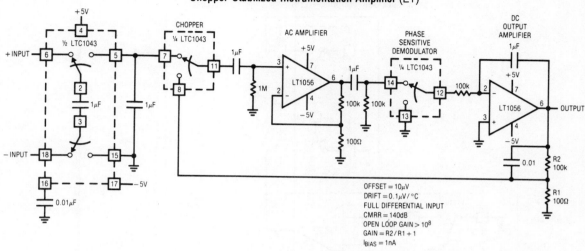

OFFSET = $10\mu V$
DRIFT = $0.1\mu V/°C$
FULL DIFFERENTIAL INPUT
CMRR = 140dB
OPEN LOOP GAIN > 10^8
GAIN = $R2/R1 + 1$
I_{BIAS} = 1nA

Lock-In Amplifier (LT)

THERMISTOR BRIDGE
IS THE SIGNAL SOURCE

SYNCHRONOUS
DEMODULATOR

TEST
POINT
A

500Hz
SINE DRIVE

T1

6.19k   6.19k

R_T

6.19k

3
+

LT1007

2
−

6

+5V

−5V

100k

100Ω

0.01   47μF

10k*   10k*

13   ¼ LTC1043

12

14   16

2
−

LM301A

3
+

+5V

−5V

8

1

30pF

1M

1μF

−
LT1012
+

+5V

−5V

6   V_{OUT} = 1000 × DC
BRIDGE SIGNAL

PHASE TRIM

50k   0.002

10k

2
+

LT1011

3
−

8

+5V

7

1

4

−5V

+5V

1k

ZERO CROSSING DETECTOR

T1 = TF5SX17ZZ, TOROTEL
R_T = YSI THERMISTOR 44006
≈ 6.19k AT 37.5°C
*MATCH 0.05%
6.19k = VISHAY S-102
OPERATE LTC1043 WITH
± 5V SUPPLIES

LOCK-IN AMPLIFIER TECHNIQUE
USED TO EXTRACT VERY SMALL SIGNALS
BURIED INTO NOISE.

39

Variable Gain Amplifier (LT)

LTC1043B

7B   8B

11B   16B ── 1kHz CLOCK

C2
100pF

12B

13B   14B

0.01

13A   LTC1043A   14A

−
A1
LT1056
+   e_OUT

12A

C1
0.01μF

11A

7A   8A   e_IN (FOR DIFFERENTIAL INPUT, GROUND PIN 8A
AND USE PINS 13A AND 7A FOR INPUTS)

16A ── f_IN 0–10kHz = GAIN 0–1000

Frequency to Voltage Converter (LT)

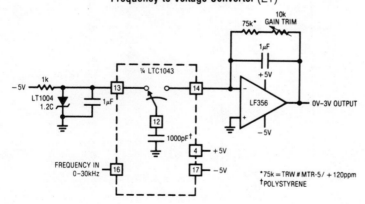

75k*   10k
GAIN TRIM

1μF

+5V

¼ LTC1043

1k
−5V
LT1004
1.2C   1μF   13   14   −
LF356
+   0V–3V OUTPUT

12
−5V

1000pF†

4   +5V

FREQUENCY IN
0–30kHz   16   17   −5V

*75k = TRW # MTR-5/ + 120ppm
†POLYSTYRENE

Linearized Platinum Signal Conditioner (LT)

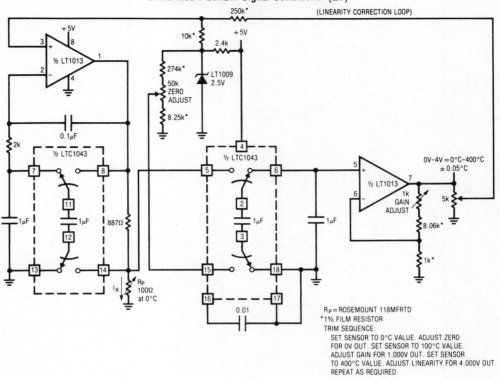

R_P = ROSEMOUNT 118MFRTD
*1% FILM RESISTOR
TRIM SEQUENCE:
SET SENSOR TO 0°C VALUE. ADJUST ZERO
FOR 0V OUT. SET SENSOR TO 100°C VALUE.
ADJUST GAIN FOR 1.000V OUT. SET SENSOR
TO 400°C VALUE. ADJUST LINEARITY FOR 4.000V OUT.
REPEAT AS REQUIRED.

Precision Current Sensing in Supply Rails (LT)

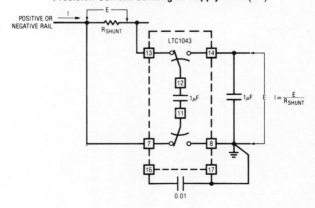

$I = \dfrac{E}{R_{SHUNT}}$

Relative Humidity Signal Conditioner (LT)

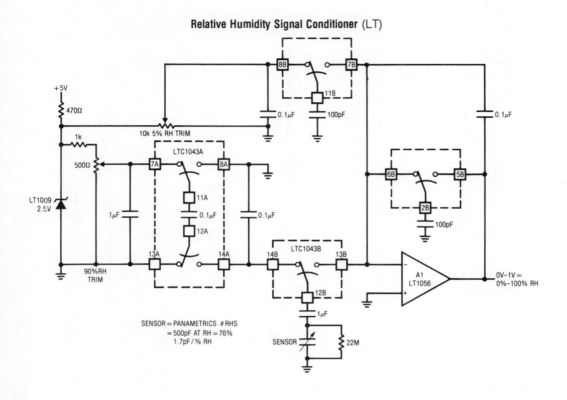

Analog Multiplier with 0.01% Accuracy (LT)

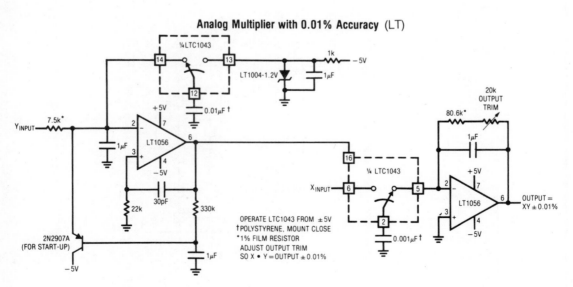

Relative Humidity Signal Conditioner (LT)

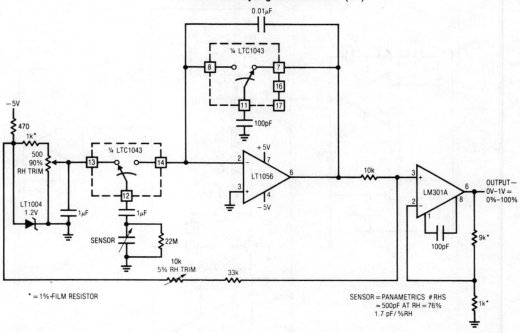

Linear Thermometer (LT)

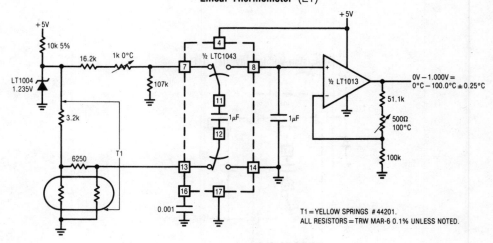

LVDT Signal Conditioner (LT)

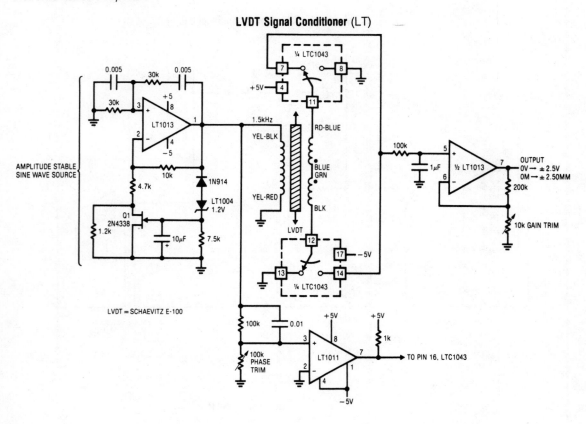

AMPLITUDE STABLE
SINE WAVE SOURCE

LVDT = SCHAEVITZ E-100

Precision Voltage Inverter (LT)

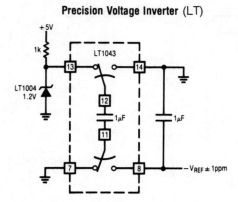

Temperature Compensated Crystal Oscillator (LT)

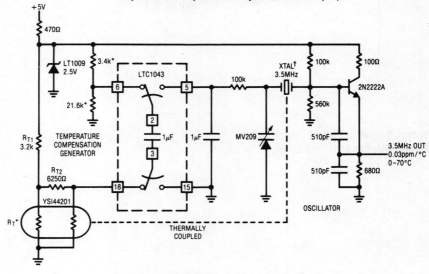

12-Bit A → D Converter (LT)

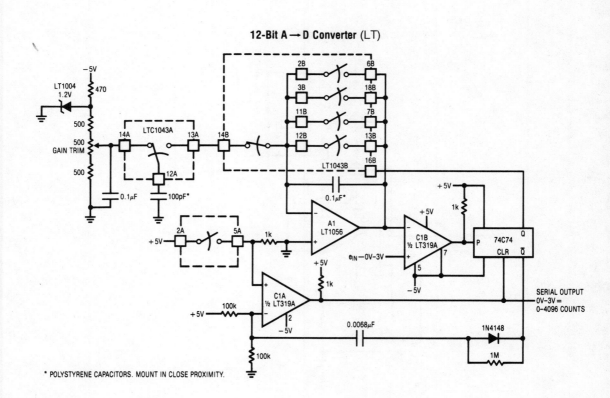

* POLYSTYRENE CAPACITORS. MOUNT IN CLOSE PROXIMITY.

Voltage Controlled Current Source with Ground Referred Input and Output (LT)

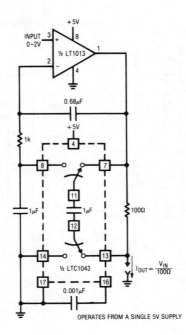

Voltage to Frequency Converter (LT)

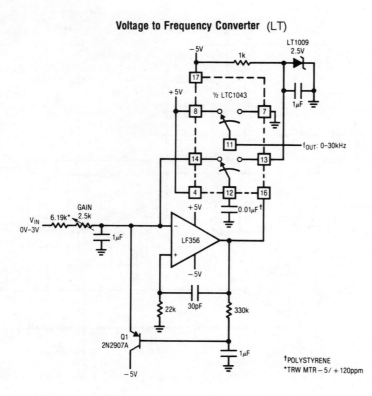

Inductorless Switching Regulator (LT)

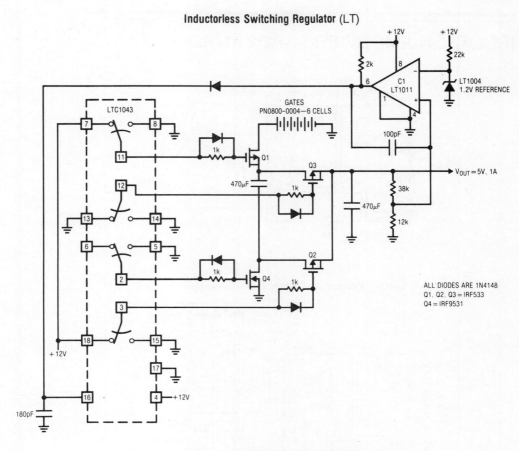

GATES
PN0800-0004—6 CELLS

ALL DIODES ARE 1N4148
Q1, Q2, Q3 = IRF533
Q4 = IRF9531

$V_{OUT} = 5V, 1A$

Instrumentation Amplifier (SIL)

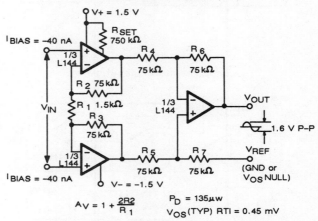

$I_{BIAS} = -40\ nA$

V_{IN}

$V_+ = 1.5\ V$

R_{SET} 750 kΩ

R_2 75 kΩ
R_1 1.5 kΩ
R_3 75 kΩ

R_4 75 kΩ
R_6 75 kΩ
R_5 75 kΩ
R_7 75 kΩ

1/3 L144

V_{OUT}

1.6 V P–P

V_{REF} (GND or V_{OS} NULL)

$V- = -1.5\ V$

$I_{BIAS} = -40\ nA$

$A_V = 1 + \dfrac{2R2}{R_1}$

$P_D = 135\mu w$
$V_{OS}(TYP)\ RTI = 0.45\ mV$

ISOLATION AMPLIFIERS—AD210 *(AD)*

Self-Powered Isolated Current Source

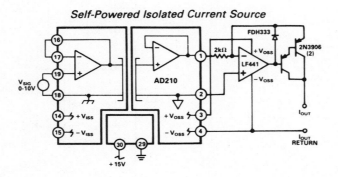

Isolated Voltage-to-Current Loop Converter

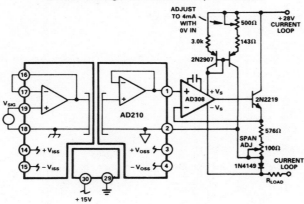

Isolated Thermocouple Amplifier

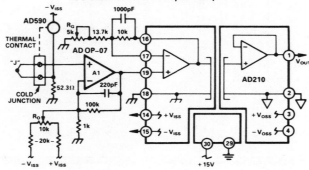

Precision Floating Programmable Reference

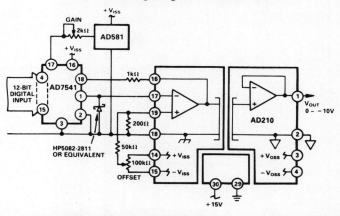

OPERATIONAL AMPLIFIERS

AD380 *(AD)*

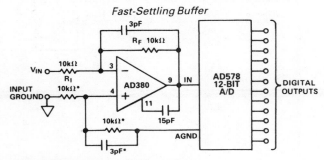

Fast-Settling Buffer

*Optional Differential Input Components Used to Reject
Noise Between Input Ground and the A/D Analog Ground.

CMOS DAC Output Amplifier

12-Bit Voltage Output DAC Circuit Settles to 1/2 LSB in 300ns

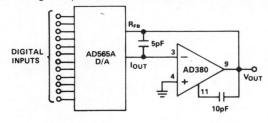

Video Amplifier

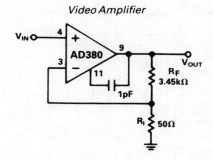

AD515A *(AD)*

Picoampere Current-to-Voltage Converter
Inverting Configuration

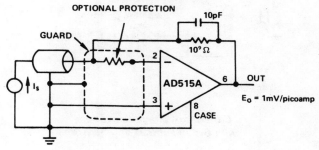

$E_O = 1mV/picoamp$

Very High Impedance Noninverting Amplifier

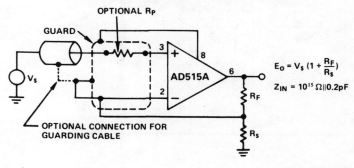

$$E_O = V_S \left(1 + \frac{R_F}{R_S}\right)$$

$$Z_{IN} = 10^{15} \, \Omega \| 0.2pF$$

Low Drift Integrator and Low-Leakage Guarded

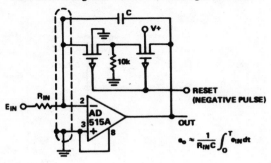

$$e_o \approx \frac{1}{R_{IN}C} \int_0^T e_{IN} dt$$

Picoampere to Voltage Converter with Gain

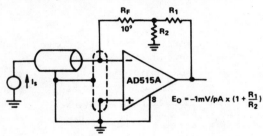

$$E_O = -1mV/pA \times \left(1 + \frac{R_1}{R_2}\right)$$

Current-to-Voltage Converters
with Grounded Bias and Sensor

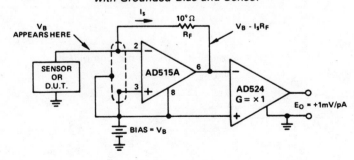

$$E_O = +1mV/pA$$

Log-Ratio Amplifier (AD)

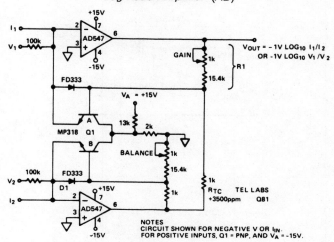

$V_{OUT} = -1V \, LOG_{10} \, I_1/I_2$
$OR \; -1V \, LOG_{10} \, V_1/V_2$

NOTES
CIRCUIT SHOWN FOR NEGATIVE V OR I_{IN}.
FOR POSITIVE INPUTS, Q1 = PNP, AND $V_A = -15V$.

Differentiator (AD)

(Differentiator schematic)

Capacitance Multiplier (AD)

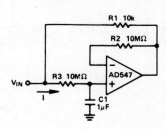

Low Drift Integrator and Low-Leakage Guarded (AD)

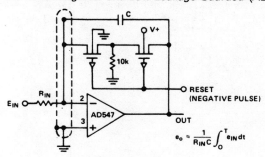

RESET
(NEGATIVE PULSE)

OUT

$$e_o \approx \frac{1}{R_{IN}C} \int_0^T e_{IN} \, dt$$

53

Long Interval Timer – 1,000 Seconds (AD)

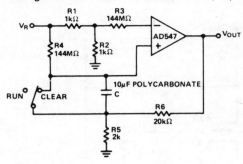

Wien-Bridge Oscillator – $f_o = 10kHz$ (AD)

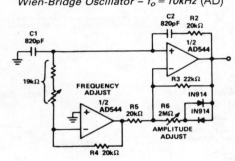

Positive Peak Detector (AD)

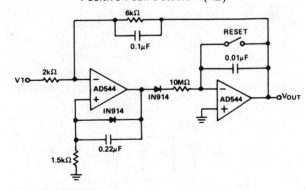

AD644 Used as DAC Output Amplifiers (AD)

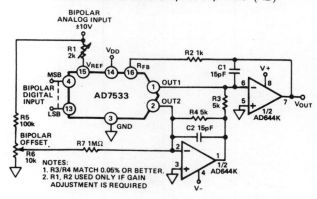

Wide Bandwidth Instrumentation Amplifier (AD)

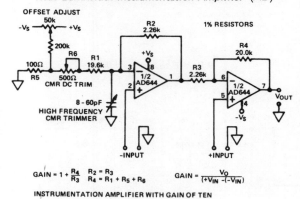

$$\text{GAIN} = 1 + \frac{R_4}{R_3} \qquad \begin{array}{l} R_2 = R_3 \\ R_4 = R_1 + R_5 + R_6 \end{array} \qquad \text{GAIN} = \frac{V_O}{(+V_{IN} - (-V_{IN})}$$

INSTRUMENTATION AMPLIFIER WITH GAIN OF TEN

Second Order Low Pass Filter (AD)

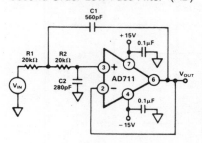

Sample and Hold Circuit (AD)

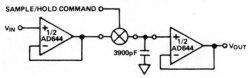

Band Pass State Variable Filter (AD)

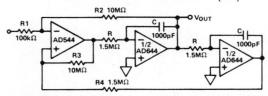

f_o = CENTER FREQUENCY = $1/2\pi$ R$_C$

Q_o = QUALITY FACTOR = $\dfrac{R_1 + R_2}{2R_1}$

H_o = GAIN AT RESONANCE = R_2/R_1

$R_3 = R_4 \approx 10^8/f_o$

Q_o, IS ADJUSTABLE BY VARYING R2
fo, IS ADJUSTABLE BY VARYING R OR C

9 Pole Chebychev Filter (AD)

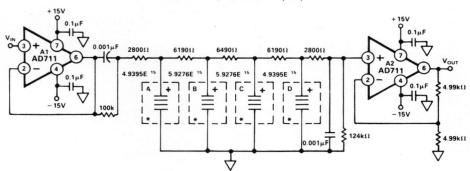

FDNR for 9 Pole Chebychev Filter (AD)

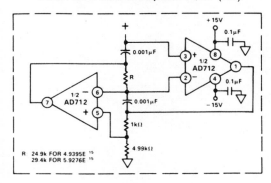

R 24.9k FOR 4.9395E ^{15}
29.4k FOR 5.9276E ^{15}

**Inverting Amplifier Model Showing
Both Lead and Lag Compensation** (AD)

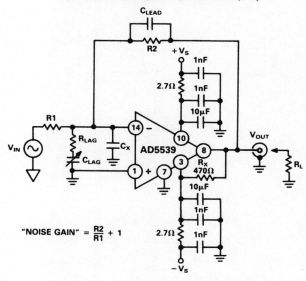

$$\text{"NOISE GAIN"} = \frac{R2}{R1} + 1$$

High Speed Peak Detector (AD)

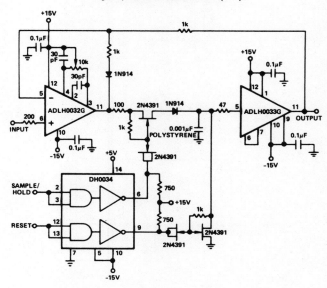

Coaxial Cable Drive (AD)

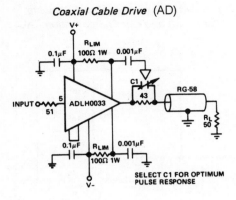

High Speed Shield/Line Driver (AD)

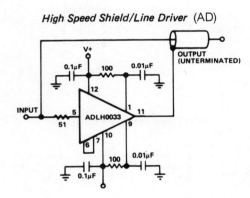

Wideband Two Pole High Pass Filter (AD)

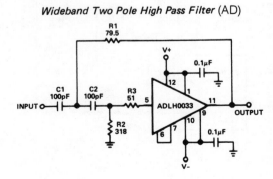

**A Model of the Feedback
Network of the Inverting Amplifier**

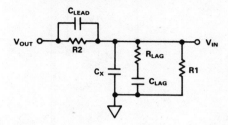

LF355, LF356, LF357, LF355B, LF356B, LF357B (MO)

DRIVING CAPACITIVE LOADS

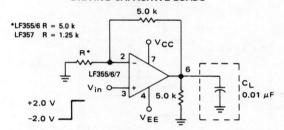

Due to a unique output stage design these amplifiers have the
ability to drive large capacitive loads and still maintain stability.
$C_{L(max)} \cong 0.01\ \mu F$.
Overshoot $\leqslant$ 20%
Settling time (t_s) $\cong$ 5.0 μs

INVERTING UNITY GAIN FOR LF357

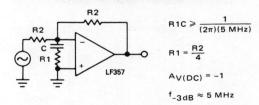

$$R1C \geqslant \frac{1}{(2\pi)(5\ \text{MHz})}$$

$$R1 = \frac{R2}{4}$$

$$A_{V(DC)} = -1$$

$$f_{-3dB} \approx 5\ \text{MHz}$$

LARGE POWER BANDWIDTH AMPLIFIER

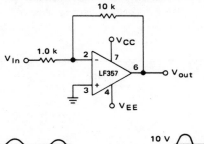

For distortion < 1% and a 20 Vp-p V_{Out}
swing, power bandwidth is: 500 kHz.

SETTLING TIME TEST CIRCUIT

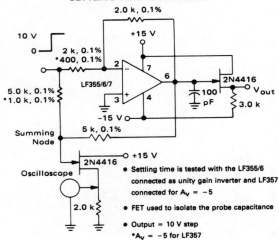

- Settling time is tested with the LF355/6 connected as unity gain inverter and LF357 connected for $A_V = -5$
- FET used to isolate the probe capacitance
- Output = 10 V step
- *$A_V = -5$ for LF357

NONINVERTING UNITY GAIN OPERATION FOR LF357

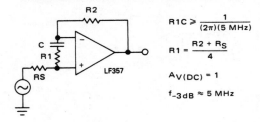

$$R1C \geq \frac{1}{(2\pi)(5 \text{ MHz})}$$

$$R1 = \frac{R2 + R_S}{4}$$

$$A_{V(DC)} = 1$$

$$f_{-3dB} \approx 5 \text{ MHz}$$

INPUT OFFSET VOLTAGE ADJUSTMENT

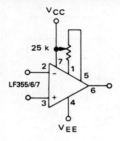

- V_{IO} is adjusted with a 25 k potentiometer
- The potentiometer wiper is connected to V_{CC}
- For potentiometers with temperature coefficient of 100 ppm/°C or less the additional drift with adjust is $\approx$ 0.5 μV/°C/mV of adjustment.
- Typical overall drift: 5.0 μV/°C $\pm$(0.5 μV/°C/mV of adjustment.)

8-BIT D/A WITH OUTPUT CURRENT
TO VOLTAGE CONVERSION

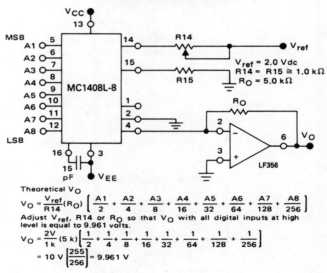

V_{ref} = 2.0 Vdc
R14 = R15 $\cong$ 1.0 kΩ
R_O = 5.0 kΩ

Theoretical V_O

$$V_O = \frac{V_{ref}}{R14}(R_O)\left[\frac{A1}{2} + \frac{A2}{4} + \frac{A3}{8} + \frac{A4}{16} + \frac{A5}{32} + \frac{A6}{64} + \frac{A7}{128} + \frac{A8}{256}\right]$$

Adjust V_{ref}, R14 or R_O so that V_O with all digital inputs at high level is equal to 9.961 volts.

$$V_O = \frac{2V}{1k}(5\,k)\left[\frac{1}{2} + \frac{1}{4} + \frac{1}{8} + \frac{1}{16} + \frac{1}{32} + \frac{1}{64} + \frac{1}{128} + \frac{1}{256}\right]$$

$$= 10\,V\left[\frac{255}{256}\right] = 9.961\,V$$

WIDE BW, LOW NOISE, LOW DRIFT AMPLIFIER

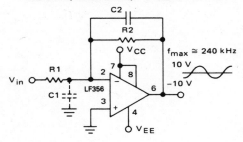

- Power BW: $f_{max} = \dfrac{S_r}{2\pi V_p} \cong 240 \text{ kHz}$

- Parasitic input capacitance (C1 $\cong$ 3 pF for LF355, LF356, and LF357 plus any additional layout capacitance) interacts with feedback elements and creates undesirable high frequency pole. To compensate add C2 such that: R2C2 $\cong$ R1C1.

ISOLATING LARGE CAPACITIVE LOADS

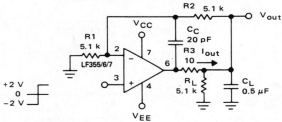

- Overshoot 6%
- $t_s = 10 \mu s$
- When driving large C_L, the V_{out} slew rate is determined by C_L and $I_{out(max)}$:

$$\frac{\Delta V_{out}}{\Delta t} = \frac{I_{out}}{C_L} \cong \frac{0.02}{0.5} \text{ V}/\mu s = 0.04 \text{ V}/\mu s \text{ (with } C_L \text{ shown)}$$

PRECISION CURRENT MONITOR

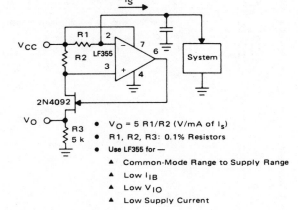

- V_O = 5 R1/R2 (V/mA of I_s)
- R1, R2, R3: 0.1% Resistors
- Use LF355 for —
  - ▲ Common-Mode Range to Supply Range
  - ▲ Low I_{IB}
  - ▲ Low V_{IO}
  - ▲ Low Supply Current

LONG INTERVAL RC TIMER

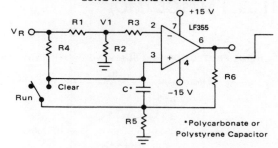

Time (t) = $R4C\ln(V_R/V_R-V_I)$, $R_3 = R_4$, $R_5 = 0.1 R_6$

If R1 = R2: t = 0.693 R4C

Design Example: 100 Second Timer

V_R = 10 V   C = 1 μF   R3 = R4 = 144 M

R6 = 20 k   R5 = 2 k   R1 = R2 = 1 k

HIGH IMPEDANCE, LOW DRIFT INSTRUMENTATION AMPLIFIER

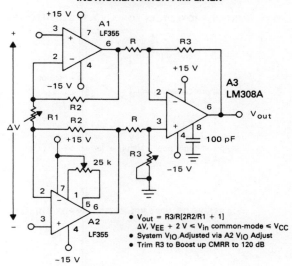

- V_{out} = R3/R[2R2/R1 + 1]
  ΔV, V_{EE} + 2 V $\leq$ V_{in} common-mode $\leq$ V_{CC}
- System V_{IO} Adjusted via A2 V_{IO} Adjust
- Trim R3 to Boost up CMRR to 120 dB

LM11, LM11C, LM11CL *(MO)*

INPUT PROTECTION FOR SUMMING (INVERTING) AMPLIFIER

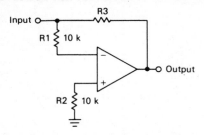

Current is limited by R1 in the event the input is connected to a low impedance source outside the common-mode range of the device. Current is controlled by R2 if one supply reverses. R1 and R2 do not affect normal operation.

INPUT PROTECTION FOR A VOLTAGE FOLLOWER

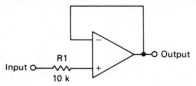

Input current is limited by R1 when the input exceeds supply voltage, power supply is turned off, or output is shorted.

CABLE BOOT STRAPPING AND INPUT SHIELDS

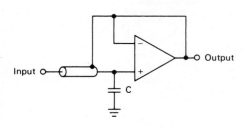

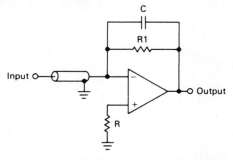

An input shield boot strapped in a voltage follower reduces input capacitance, leakage, and spurious voltages from cable flexing. A small capacitor from the input to ground will prevent any instability.

In a summing amplifier the input is at virtual ground. Therefore the shield can be grounded. A small feedback capacitor will insure stability.

ADJUSTING INPUT OFFSET VOLTAGE WITH BALANCE POTENTIOMETER

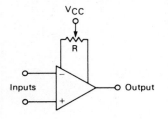

Minimum Adjustment Range (mV)	R Ω
± 0.4	1.0 k
± 1.0	3.0 k
± 2.0	10 k
± 5.0	100 k

Input offset voltage adjustment range is a function of the Balance Potentiometer Resistance as indicated by the table above. The potentiometer is connected between the two "Balance" pins.

GUARD RING ELECTRICAL CONNECTIONS
FOR COMMON AMPLIFIER CONFIGURATIONS

Summing Amp (Inverting)

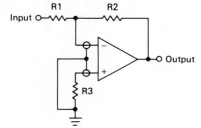

Non-Inverting

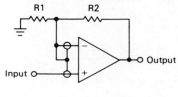

Voltage Follower

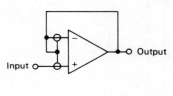

ZERO-CROSSING DETECTOR
DRIVING CMOS LOGIC

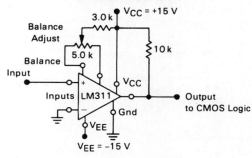

RELAY DRIVER WITH STROBE CAPABILITY

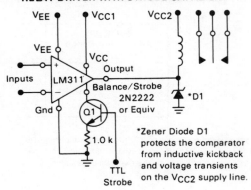

*Zener Diode D1 protects the comparator from inductive kickback and voltage transients on the V_{CC2} supply line.

LM124, LM224, LM324A, LM2902 *(MO)*

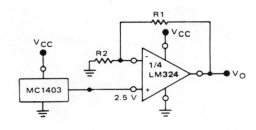

$$V_O = 2.5\,V\left(1 + \frac{R1}{R2}\right)$$

WIEN BRIDGE OSCILLATOR

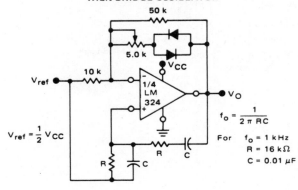

$$f_o = \frac{1}{2\pi RC}$$

$$V_{ref} = \frac{1}{2}\,V_{CC}$$

For $f_o = 1\,kHz$
$R = 16\,k\Omega$
$C = 0.01\,\mu F$

HIGH IMPEDANCE DIFFERENTIAL AMPLIFIER

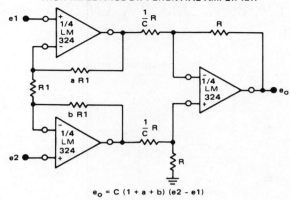

$$e_O = C\,(1 + a + b)\,(e2 - e1)$$

COMPARATOR WITH HYSTERESIS

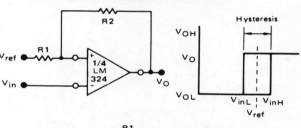

$$V_{inL} = \frac{R1}{R1 + R2}\,(V_{OL} - V_{ref}) + V_{ref}$$

$$V_{inH} = \frac{R1}{R1 + R2}\,(V_{OH} - V_{ref}) + V_{ref}$$

$$H = \frac{R1}{R1 + R2}\,(V_{OH} - V_{OL})$$

BI-QUAD FILTER

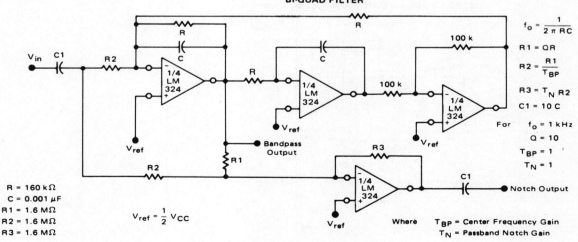

$$f_O = \frac{1}{2\pi RC}$$

$$R1 = QR$$

$$R2 = \frac{R1}{T_{BP}}$$

$$R3 = T_N\,R2$$

$$C1 = 10\,C$$

For $f_O = 1\,kHz$

$Q = 10$

$T_{BP} = 1$

$T_N = 1$

R = 160 kΩ
C = 0.001 μF
R1 = 1.6 MΩ
R2 = 1.6 MΩ
R3 = 1.6 MΩ

$$V_{ref} = \frac{1}{2}\,V_{CC}$$

Where T_{BP} = Center Frequency Gain
T_N = Passband Notch Gain

67

LM139,A, LM239,A, LM339,A, LM2901, MC3302 *(MO)*

DRIVING LOGIC

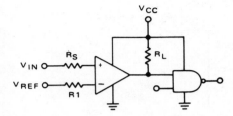

R_S = Source Resistance
$R1 \simeq R_S$

LOGIC	DEVICE	V_{CC} Volts	R_L $k\Omega$
CMOS	1/4 MC14001	+15	100
TTL	1/4 MC7400	+5	10

ZERO CROSSING DETECTOR (Split Supplies)

$V_{INmin} \approx 0.4$ V peak for 1% phase distortion ($\Delta(\cdot)$).

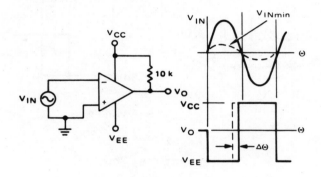

ZERO CROSSING DETECTOR (Single Supply)

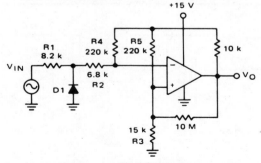

D1 prevents input from going negative by more than 0.6 V.

R1 + R2 = R3

$R3 \leqslant \dfrac{R5}{10}$ for small error in zero crossing

SQUAREWAVE OSCILLATOR

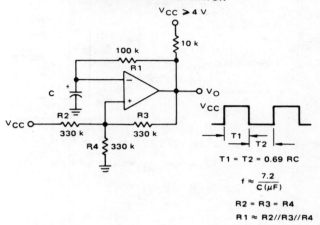

$$T1 = T2 = 0.69 \, RC$$

$$f \approx \frac{7.2}{C \, (\mu F)}$$

$$R2 = R3 = R4$$

$$R1 \approx R2 // R3 // R4$$

LM148 *(MO)*

WIEN BRIDGE OSCILLATOR

$V_{ref} = \frac{1}{2} \, V_{CC}$

$$f_o = \frac{1}{2 \pi \, RC}$$

For $f_o = 1 \, kHz$
  $R = 16 \, k\Omega$
  $C = 0.01 \, \mu F$

COMPARATOR WITH HYSTERESIS

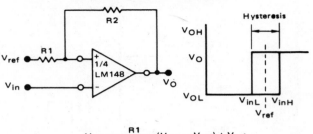

$$V_{inL} = \frac{R1}{R1 + R2} (V_{OL} - V_{ref}) + V_{ref}$$

$$V_{inH} = \frac{R1}{R1 + R2} (V_{OH} - V_{ref}) + V_{ref}$$

$$H = \frac{R1}{R1 + R2} (V_{OH} - V_{OL})$$

HIGH IMPEDANCE DIFFERENTIAL AMPLIFIER

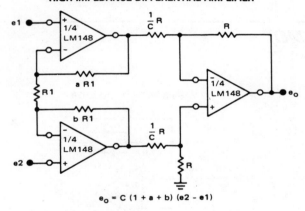

$$e_o = C (1 + a + b) (e2 - e1)$$

VOLTAGE REFERENCE

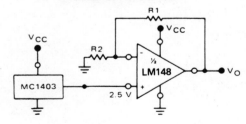

$$V_O \quad 2.5 \, V (1 + \frac{R1}{R2})$$

BI-QUAD FILTER

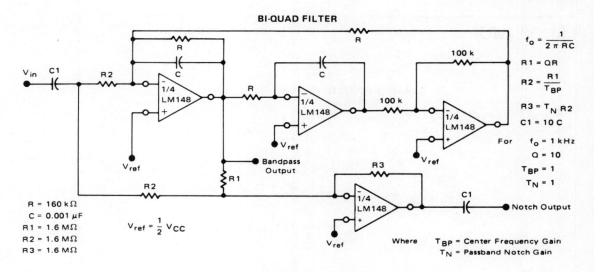

$$f_o = \frac{1}{2\pi RC}$$

$$R1 = QR$$

$$R2 = \frac{R1}{T_{BP}}$$

$$R3 = T_N R2$$

$$C1 = 10 C$$

For $\quad f_o = 1\,kHz$

$\qquad Q = 10$

$\qquad T_{BP} = 1$

$\qquad T_N = 1$

$R = 160\,k\Omega$
$C = 0.001\,\mu F$
$R1 = 1.6\,M\Omega$
$R2 = 1.6\,M\Omega$
$R3 = 1.6\,M\Omega$

$$V_{ref} = \frac{1}{2} V_{CC}$$

Where T_{BP} = Center Frequency Gain
$\qquad\quad T_N$ = Passband Notch Gain

HIGH IMPEDANCE INSTRUMENTATION BUFFER/FILTER

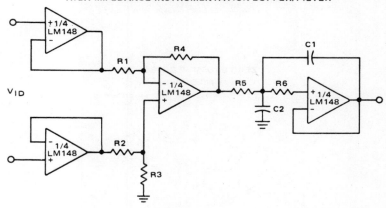

FUNCTION GENERATOR

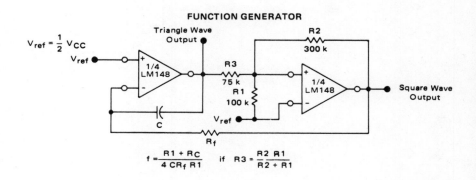

$$f = \frac{R1 + RC}{4\,CR_f\,R1} \qquad if \quad R3 = \frac{R2\,R1}{R2 + R1}$$

71

LM193 *(MO)*

ZERO CROSSING DETECTOR
(Single Supply)

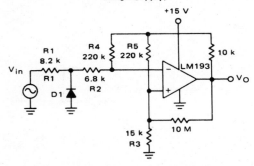

D1 prevents input from going negative by more than 0.6 V.

$$R1 + R2 = R3$$

$$R3 \leqslant \frac{R5}{10} \text{ for small error in zero crossing}$$

ZERO CROSSING DETECTOR
(Split Supplies)

$V_{INmin} \approx 0.4$ V peak for 1% phase distortion ($\triangle \Theta$).

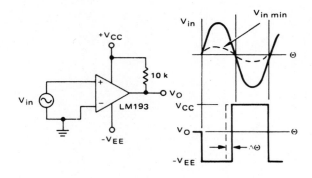

FREE-RUNNING SQUARE-WAVE OSCILLATOR

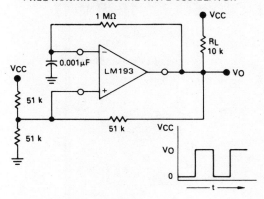

TIME DELAY GENERATOR

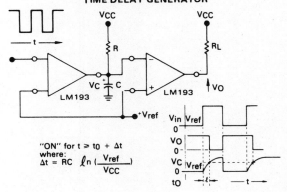

"ON" for t ≥ $t_0 + \Delta t$
where:
$\Delta t = RC \ \ell n \left(\dfrac{V_{ref}}{V_{CC}} \right)$

COMPARATOR WITH HYSTERESIS

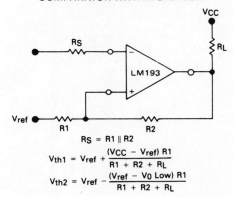

$R_S = R1 \parallel R2$

$$V_{th1} = V_{ref} + \frac{(V_{CC} - V_{ref})\,R1}{R1 + R2 + R_L}$$

$$V_{th2} = V_{ref} - \frac{(V_{ref} - V_0\,Low)\,R1}{R1 + R2 + R_L}$$

73

MC1436, MC1436C, MC1536 *(MO)*

INVERTING FEEDBACK MODEL

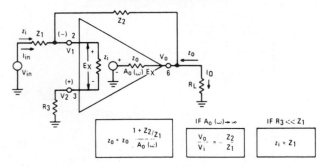

$$z_0 = z_0 \frac{1 + Z_2/Z_1}{A_0(\omega)}$$

IF $A_0(\omega) \to \infty$

$$\frac{V_0}{V_i} = -\frac{Z_2}{Z_1}$$

IF $R_3 \ll Z_1$

$$z_i \approx Z_1$$

NON-INVERTING FEEDBACK MODEL

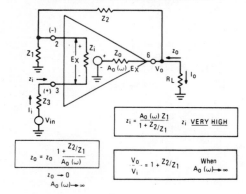

$$z_i = \frac{A_0(\omega) Z_1}{1 + Z_2/Z_1} \quad z_i \text{ VERY HIGH}$$

$$z_0 = z_0 \frac{1 + Z_2/Z_1}{A_0(\omega)}$$

$$z_0 \to 0$$
$$A_0(\omega) \to \infty$$

$$\frac{V_0}{V_i} = 1 + Z_2/Z_1 \quad \begin{array}{l}\text{When}\\ A_0(\omega) \to \infty\end{array}$$

VOLTAGE CONTROLLED CURRENT SOURCE or TRANSCONDUCTANCE AMPLIFIER WITH 0 TO 40 V COMPLIANCE

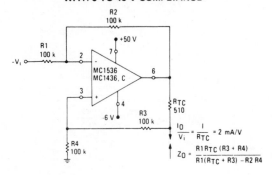

$$\frac{I_0}{V_i} = \frac{1}{R_{TC}} = 2 \text{ mA/V}$$

$$Z_0 = \frac{R1 R_{TC} (R3 + R4)}{R1(R_{TC} + R3) - R2 R4}$$

AUDIO AMPLIFIER

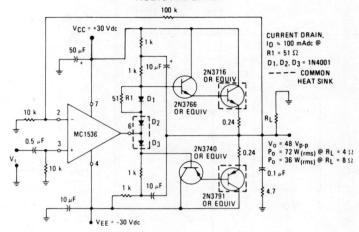

MC1439, MC1539 *(MO)*

DIFFERENTIAL AMPLIFIER

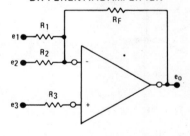

$$e_0 = - \left| \frac{R_F}{R_1} e1 + \frac{R_F}{R_2} e2 \right| + \left| 1 + \frac{R_F}{R_3} \right| e3$$

$$\text{For } R_3 = \frac{R_1, R_2}{R_1 + R_2}$$

*Properly Compensated

VOLTAGE FOLLOWER

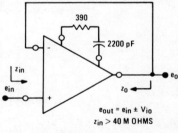

$e_{out} = e_{in} \pm V_{io}$

$z_{in} > 40$ M OHMS

$$z_{oCL} = z_{oOL} \left[\frac{1 + \frac{R_F}{R_i}}{A_{ol}} \right] = 4 \text{ k} \left[\frac{1 + 0}{10^5} \right] \approx 0.04 \text{ OHM}$$

+15 VOLT REGULATOR

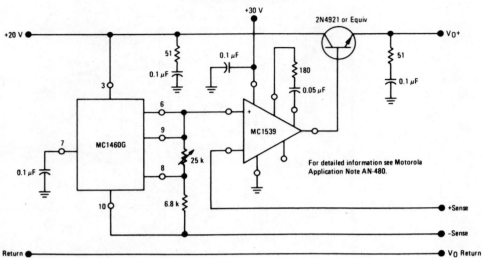

For detailed information see Motorola
Application Note AN-480.

SUMMING AMPLIFIER

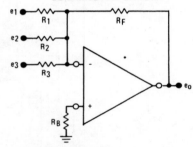

R_B = Parallel Combination of R_1, R_2, R_3, R_F.

$$e_0 = - \left| \frac{R_F}{R_1} e1 + \frac{R_F}{R_2} e2 + \frac{R_F}{R_3} e3 \right|$$

*Properly Compensated

MC1456, MC1456C, MC1556 *(MO)*

TYPICAL APPLICATIONS

Where values are not given for external components they must be selected by the designer to fit the requirements of the system.

INVERTING FEEDBACK MODEL

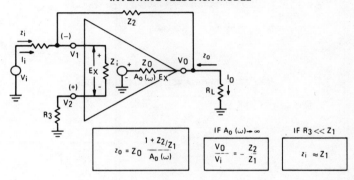

$$z_0 = Z_0 \; \frac{1 + Z_2/Z_1}{A_0(\omega)}$$

IF $A_0(\omega) \rightarrow \infty$

$$\frac{V_0}{V_i} = -\frac{Z_2}{Z_1}$$

IF $R_3 \ll Z_1$

$$z_i \approx Z_1$$

NONINVERTING FEEDBACK MODEL

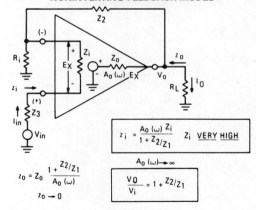

$$z_i = \frac{A_0(\omega) \; Z_i}{1 + Z_2/Z_1} \qquad Z_i \; \underline{VERY \; HIGH}$$

$A_0(\omega) \rightarrow \infty$

$$\frac{V_0}{V_i} = 1 + Z_2/Z_1$$

$$z_0 = Z_0 \; \frac{1 + Z_2/Z_1}{A_0(\omega)}$$

$$z_0 \rightarrow 0$$

W-DRIFT SAMPLE AND HOLD

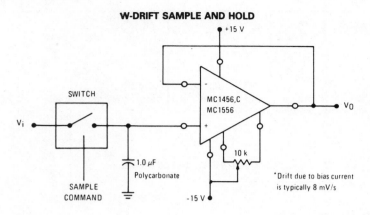

HIGH IMPEDANCE BRIDGE AMPLIFIER

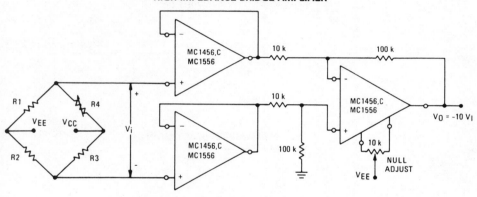

LOGARITHMIC AMPLIFIER

$$V_O = K_1 \ln (K_2 V_i)$$

VOLTAGE OFFSET NULL CIRCUIT

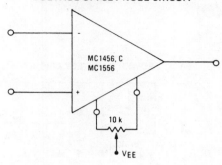

12.5-WATT WIDEBAND POWER AMPLIFIER

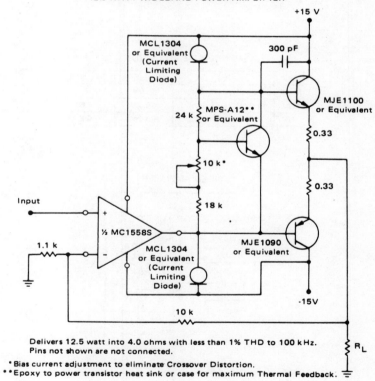

Delivers 12.5 watt into 4.0 ohms with less than 1% THD to 100 kHz.
Pins not shown are not connected.

* Bias current adjustment to eliminate Crossover Distortion.
** Epoxy to power transistor heat sink or case for maximum Thermal Feedback.

MC1400P *(MO)*

60 MHz POWER GAIN TEST CIRCUIT

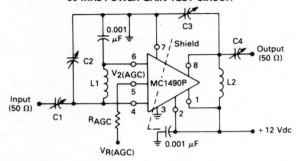

L1 = 7 Turns, #20 AWG Wire, 5/16" Dia.,   C1,C2,C3 = (1–30) pF
     5/8" Long   C4 = (1–10) pF
L2 = 6 Turns, #14 AWG Wire, 9/16" Dia.,
     3/4" Long

PROCEDURE FOR SETUP

Test	e_{in}	$V_{2(AGC)}$	R_{AGC}(kΩ)
M_{AGC}	2.23 mV (−40 dBm)	5–7 V	0
G_p	1.0 mV (−47 dBm)	≤5.0 V	5.6
NF	1.0 mV (−47 dBm)	≤5.0 V	5.6

VIDEO AMPLIFIER

30 MHz AMPLIFIER
(Power Gain = 50 dB, BW ≈ 1.0 MHz)

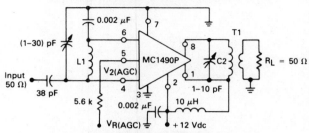

L1 = 12 Turns #22 AWG Wire on a Toroid Core,
(T37-6 Micro Metal or Equiv)
T1: Primary = 17 Turns #20 AWG Wire on a Toroid Core,
(T44-6)
Secondary = 2 Turns #20 AWG Wire

100 MHz MIXER

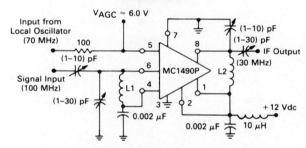

L1 = 5 Turns, #16 AWG Wire, 1/4" ID,
5/8" Long
L2 = 16 Turns, #20 AWG Wire on a Toroid
Core, (T44–6)

CA3078, CA3078A *(RCA)*

Offset voltage null circuits.

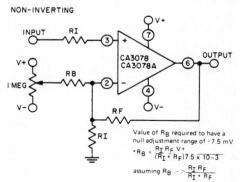

NON-INVERTING

Value of R_B required to have a
null adjustment range of ·7.5 mV

$$R_B \approx \frac{R_I R_F V+}{(R_I + R_F)7.5 \times 10^{-3}}$$

assuming $R_B > \frac{R_I R_F}{R_I + R_F}$

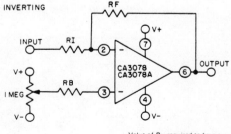

INVERTING

Value of R_B required to have a
null adjustment range of ·7.5 mV

$$R_B \approx \frac{R_I V+}{7.5 \times 10^{-3}}$$

assuming $R_B > > R_I$

Inverting 20-dB amplifier circuit.

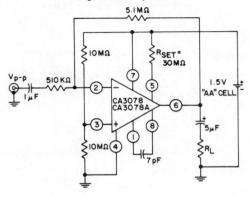

Non inverting 20-dB amplifier circuit.

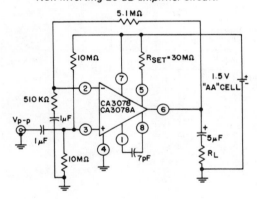

CA3080, CA3080A *(RCA)*

*Thermocouple temperature
control with CA3079 zero voltage switch as the output amplifier.*

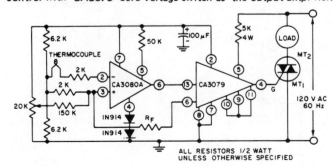

1,000,000/1 single-control function generator — 1 MHz to 1 Hz.

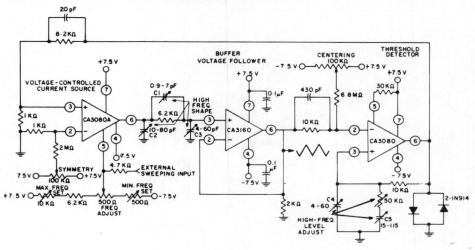

Schematic diagram of the CA3080A in a sample-hold configuration.

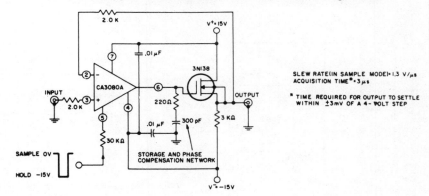

Sample and hold circuit.

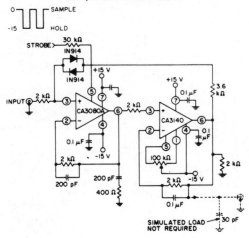

CA3094, CA3094A, CA3094B *(RCA)*

RC timer triggered by external negative pulse.

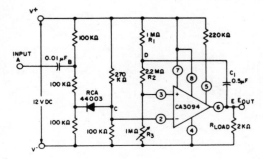

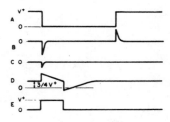

On a negative-going transient at input (A), a negative pulse at C will turn "on" the CA3094, and the output (E) will go from a low to a high level.

At the end of the time constant determined by C_1, R_1, R_2, R_3, the CA3094 will return to the "off" state and the output will be pulled low by R_{LOAD}. This condition will be independent of the interval when input A returns to a high level.

Free-running pulse generator.

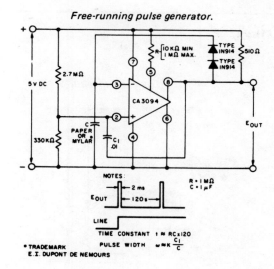

Current or voltage-controlled oscillator.

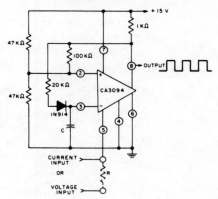

Single-supply astable multivibrator.

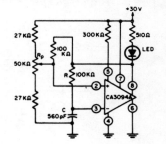

Dual-supply astable multivibrator.

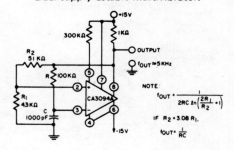

CA3100 (RCA)

20 dB video line driver.

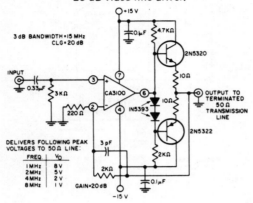

1 MHz meter-driver amplifier.

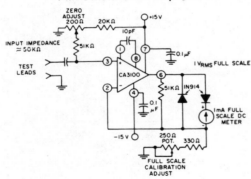

20 dB video amplifier.

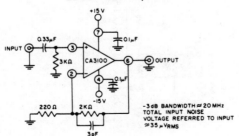

Fast positive peak detector.

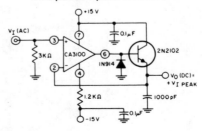

CA3130, CA3130A *(RCA)*

*Single-supply, absolute-value, ideal full-wave
rectifier with associated waveforms.*

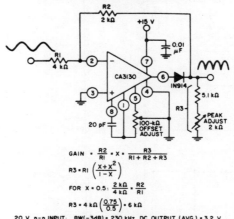

$$\text{GAIN} = \frac{R2}{R1} = X = \frac{R3}{R1 + R2 + R3}$$

$$R3 = R1\left(\frac{X + X^2}{1 - X}\right)$$

$$\text{FOR } X = 0.5: \quad \frac{2 \text{ k}\Omega}{4 \text{ k}\Omega} = \frac{R2}{R1}$$

$$R3 = 4 \text{ k}\Omega\left(\frac{0.75}{0.5}\right) = 6 \text{ k}\Omega$$

20 V p-p INPUT: BW(-3dB) = 230 kHz, DC OUTPUT (AVG.) = 3.2 V
1 VOLT p-p INPUT: BW(-3dB) = 130 kHz, DC OUTPUT (AVG.) = 160 mV

*Function generator (frequency can be varied
1,000,000/1 with a single control).*

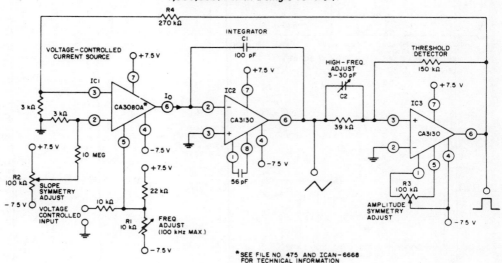

*SEE FILE NO. 475 AND ICAN-6668
FOR TECHNICAL INFORMATION

Voltage regulator circuit (0 to 13 V at 40 mA).

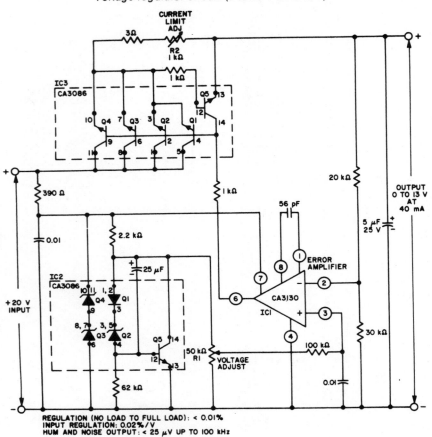

REGULATION (NO LOAD TO FULL LOAD): < 0.01%
INPUT REGULATION: 0.02%/V
HUM AND NOISE OUTPUT: < 25 µV UP TO 100 kHz

Peak-detector circuits.

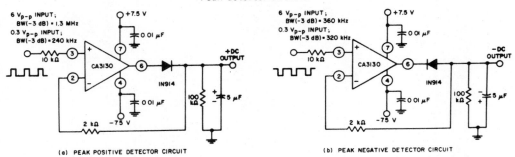

(a) PEAK POSITIVE DETECTOR CIRCUIT   (b) PEAK NEGATIVE DETECTOR CIRCUIT

CMOS transistor array (CA3600E) connected as power-booster in the output stage of the CA3130.

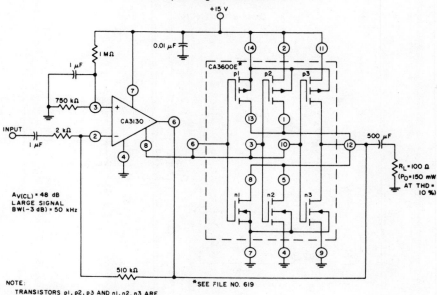

$A_{V(CL)} = 48$ dB
LARGE SIGNAL
BW(-3 dB) $= 50$ kHz

NOTE:

TRANSISTORS pl, p2, p3 AND nl, n2, n3 ARE
PARALLEL-CONNECTED WITH Q8 AND Q12,
RESPECTIVELY, OF THE CA3130

*SEE FILE NO. 619

Voltage regulator circuit (0.1 to 50 V at 1 A).

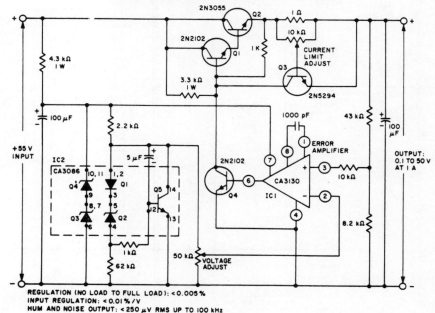

REGULATION (NO LOAD TO FULL LOAD): < 0.005 %
INPUT REGULATION: < 0.01 %/V
HUM AND NOISE OUTPUT: < 250 μV RMS UP TO 100 kHz

CA3240 (RCA)

Dual level detector.

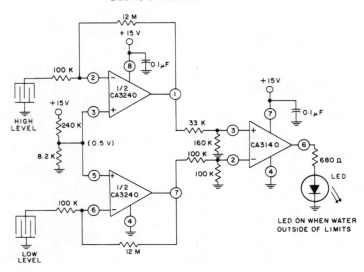

Constant-voltage/constant-current power supply.

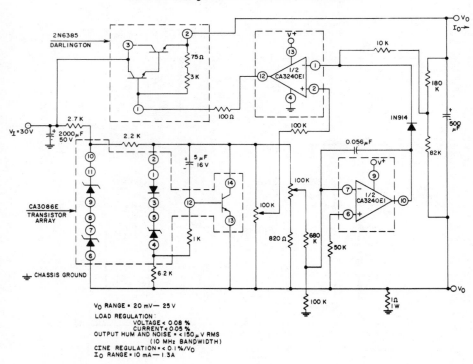

V_O RANGE = 20 mV — 25 V
LOAD REGULATION:
    VOLTAGE < 0.08 %
    CURRENT < 0.05 %
OUTPUT HUM AND NOISE = < 150 μV RMS
    (10 MHz BANDWIDTH)
CINE REGULATION = < 0.1 %/V_O
I_O RANGE = 10 mA — 1.3A

CA3420 (RCA)

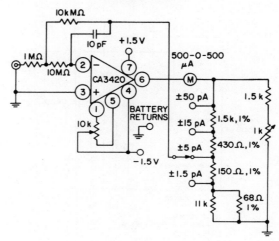

Picoameter circuit.

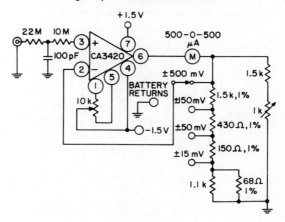

High input resistance voltmeter.

CA3440 (RCA)

High-input impedance amplifier.

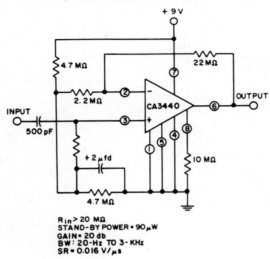

$R_{in} > 20$ MΩ
STAND-BY POWER = 90 μW
GAIN = 20 db
BW: 20-Hz TO 3-KHz
SR = 0.016 V/μs

Micropower bandgap reference.

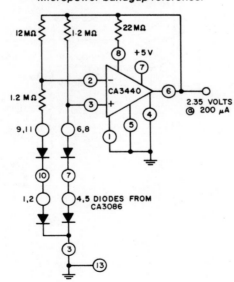

CA3493A, CA3493 *(RCA)*

Typical two-op amp bridge-type differential amplifier.

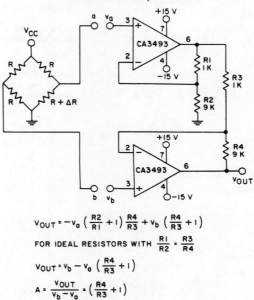

$$V_{OUT} = -v_a \left(\frac{R2}{R1} + 1 \right) \frac{R4}{R3} + v_b \left(\frac{R4}{R3} + 1 \right)$$

FOR IDEAL RESISTORS WITH $\frac{R1}{R2} = \frac{R3}{R4}$

$$V_{OUT} = v_b - v_a \left(\frac{R4}{R3} + 1 \right)$$

$$A = \frac{V_{OUT}}{v_b - v_a} = \left(\frac{R4}{R3} + 1 \right)$$

FOR VALUES ABOVE $V_{OUT} = (v_b - v_a)(10)$

Typical summing amplifier application.

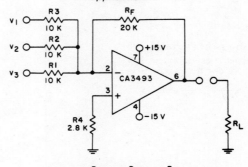

$$V_{OUT} = -\left(\frac{R_F}{R1} v_1 + \frac{R_F}{R2} v_2 + \frac{R_F}{R3} v_3 \right)$$

$$V_{OUT} = -(2 v_1 + 2 v_2 + 2 v_3)$$

ALL RESISTANCE VALUES ARE IN OHMS

93

Differential amplifier (simple subtractor) using CA3493.

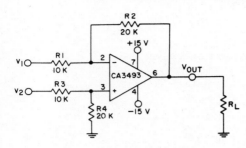

IF $R4 = R2$, $R3 = R1$ AND $\dfrac{R2}{R1} = \dfrac{R4}{R3}$

THEN $V_{OUT} = (V_2 - V_1)\left(\dfrac{R2}{R1}\right)$

FOR VALUES ABOVE $V_{OUT} = 2(V_2 - V_1)$

IF A_V IS TO BE MADE 1 AND IF $R1 = R3 = R4 = R$ WITH $R2 = 0.999\,R$ (0.1% MISMATCH IN R2)

THEN $V_{OCM} = 0.0005\ V_{IN}$ OR CMRR = 66 dB
THUS, THE CMRR OF THIS CIRCUIT IS LIMITED BY THE MATCHING OR MISMATCHING OF THIS NETWORK RATHER THAN THE AMPLIFIER.

$$V_{OUT} = V_2\left(\frac{R4}{R3+R4}\right)\left(\frac{R1+R2}{R1}\right) - V_1\left(\frac{R2}{R1}\right)$$

Using CA3493 as a bilateral current source.

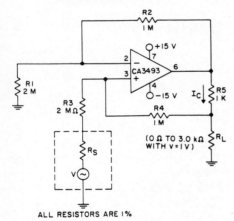

ALL RESISTORS ARE 1%

IF $R1 = R3$ AND $R2 \approx R4 + R5$ THEN

I_L IS INDEPENDENT OF VARIATIONS IN R_L FOR R_L VALUES OF 0 Ω TO 3 kΩ WITH $v = 1$ V

$$I_L = \frac{v\ R4}{R3\ R5} = \frac{v\ 1M}{(2M)(1K)} = \frac{v}{2K} = 500\ \mu A$$

LM101A/201A/301A *(RAY)*

Inverting Amplifier With Balancing Circuit

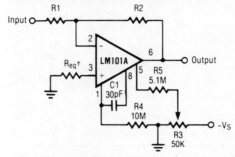

†May be zero or equal to parallel combination of R1 and R2 for minimum offset.

Voltage Comparator for Driving DTL or TTL Integrated Circuits

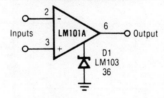

Voltage Comparator for Driving RTL Logic or High Current Driver

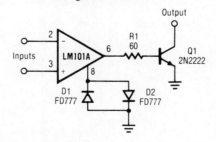

Low Drift Sample and Hold

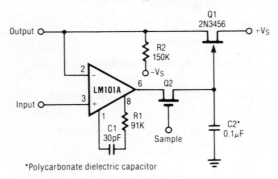

*Polycarbonate dielectric capacitor

LM148/248/348 (Low-Power Quad 741 Op Amp)
(RAY)

One Decade Low Distortion Sinewave Generator

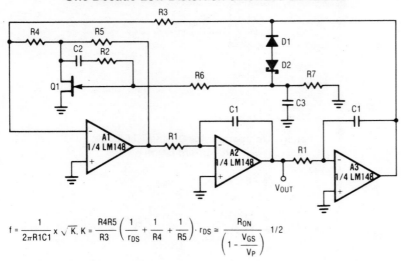

$$f = \frac{1}{2\pi R1 C1} \times \sqrt{K}, \quad K = \frac{R4 R5}{R3}\left(\frac{1}{r_{DS}} + \frac{1}{R4} + \frac{1}{R5}\right) \cdot r_{DS} \cong \frac{R_{ON}}{\left(1 - \frac{V_{GS}}{V_P}\right)} \quad 1/2$$

$f_{MAX} = 5.0\text{kHz}$, THD $\leq 0.03\%$
R1 = 100K pot., C1 = 0.0047μF, C2 = 0.01μF, C3 = 0.1μF, R2 = R6 = R7 = 1M, R3 = 5.1K, R4 = 12Ω.
R5 = 240Ω, Q1 = NS5102, D1 = 1N914, D2 = 3.6V avalanche diode (ex. LM103). $V_S = \pm15V$
A simpler version with some distortion degradation at high frequencies can be made by using A1
as a simple inverting amplifier, and by putting back to back zeners in the feedback loop of A3.

Low Cost Instrumentation Amplifier

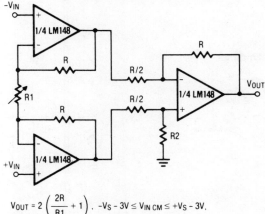

$$V_{OUT} = 2\left(\frac{2R}{R1} + 1\right), \quad -V_S - 3V \le V_{IN\,CM} \le +V_S - 3V.$$

$V_S = \pm15V$
$R = R2$, trim R2 to boost CMRR

Low Voltage Peak Detector With Bias Current Compensation

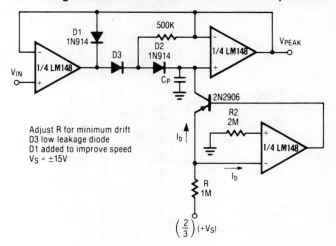

Adjust R for minimum drift
D3 low leakage diode
D1 added to improve speed
$V_S = \pm15V$

3900 (RAY)

Inverting Amplifier

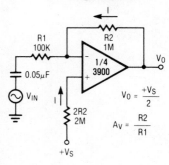

$$V_0 = \frac{+V_S}{2}$$

$$A_V = \frac{R2}{R1}$$

V_{BE} Biasing

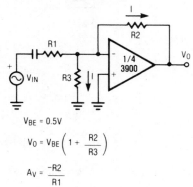

$$V_{BE} = 0.5V$$

$$V_0 = V_{BE}\left(1 + \frac{R2}{R3}\right)$$

$$A_V = \frac{-R2}{R1}$$

Voltage-Controlled Current Source
(Transconductance Amplifier)

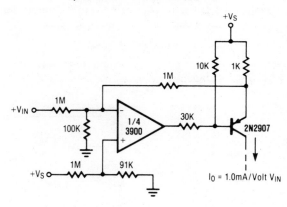

$$I_0 = 1.0mA/Volt\ V_{IN}$$

Triangle/Square Generator

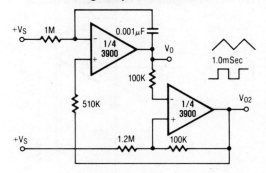

Supplying I_{IN} With Auxiliary Amplifier
(to Allow High Z Feedback Networks)

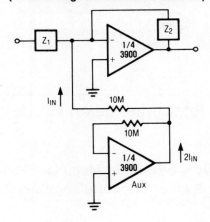

Bandpass Active Filter

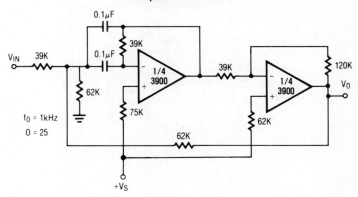

Free-Running Staircase Generator/Pulse Counter

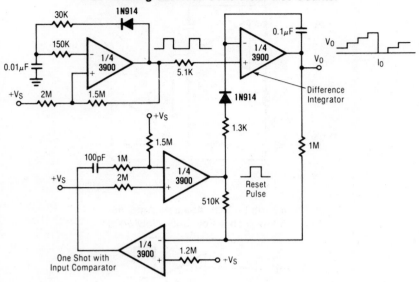

OP-05 Series (Instrumentation Grade) *(RAY)*

**Pin Outs Shown for Metal Can Packages
Except Offset Nulling Circuit**

High Speed, Low V_{OS} Composite Amplifier

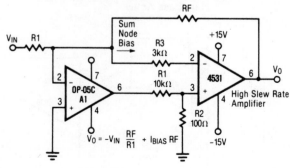

$$V_0 = -V_{IN}\frac{RF}{R1} + I_{BIAS}\,RF$$

Adjustment-Free Precision Summing Amplifier

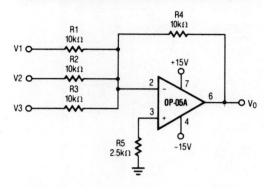

High Stability Thermocouple Amplifier

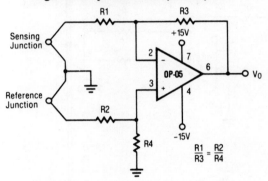

Precision Absolute Value Circuit

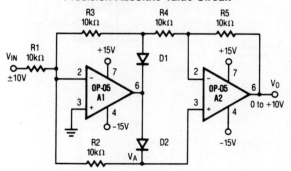

Offset Nulling Circuit

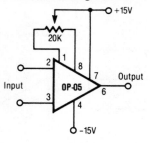

High Speed, Low V_{OS} Composite Amplifier

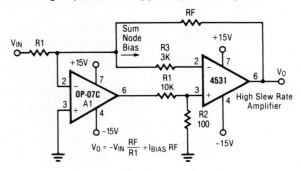

$$V_0 = -V_{IN} \frac{RF}{R1} + I_{BIAS} RF$$

High Stability Thermocouple Amplifier

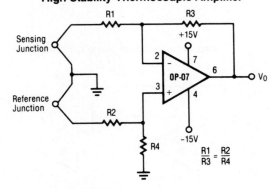

$$\frac{R1}{R3} = \frac{R2}{R4}$$

*Pin Outs Shown for Metal Can Packages

Adjustment-Free Precision Summing Amplifier

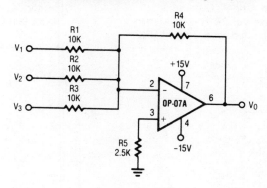

Precision Absolute Value Circuit

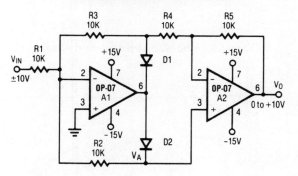

OP-27 (Very Low Noise) *(RAY)*

Low Impedance Microphone Preamplifier

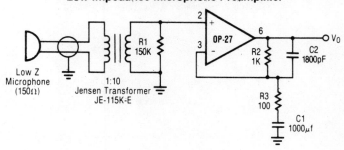

A Single Op Amp IC Difference Amplifier Using an OP-27. The Difference Amplifier is Connected for a Gain of 1000.

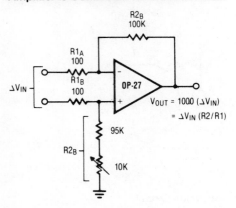

$V_{OUT} = 1000 \, (\Delta V_{IN})$
$= \Delta V_{IN} \, (R2/R1)$

Common Mode Rejection Ratio Test Circuit

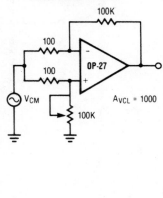

$A_{VCL} = 1000$

Three Op Amp IC Instrumentation Amplifier

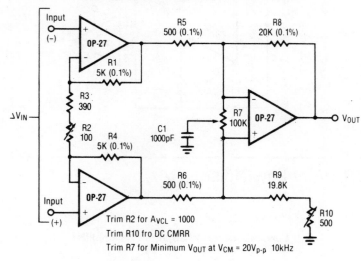

Trim R2 for $A_{VCL} = 1000$
Trim R10 fro DC CMRR
Trim R7 for Minimum V_{OUT} at $V_{CM} = 20V_{p-p}$ 10kHz

OP-37 *(RAY)*

A Single Op Amp IC Difference Amplifier Using an OP-37.
The Difference Amplifier is Connected for a Gain of 1000.

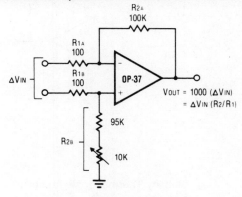

Common Mode Rejection Ratio Test Circuit

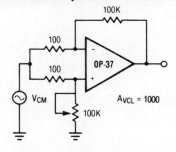

714 *(RAY)*

High Speed, Low V_{OS} Composite Amplifier

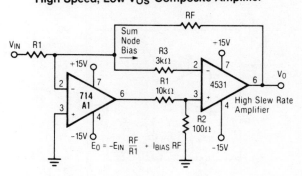

Adjustment-Free Precision Summing Amplifier

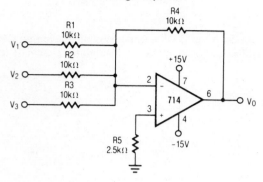

High Stability Thermocouple Amplifier

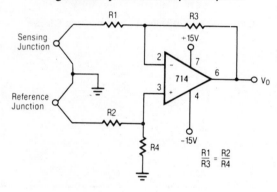

$$\frac{R1}{R3} = \frac{R2}{R4}$$

Precision Absolute Value Circuit

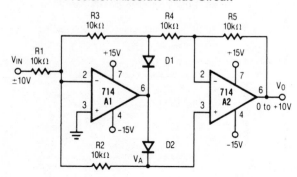

RC747/747S *(RAY)*

Quadrature Oscillator

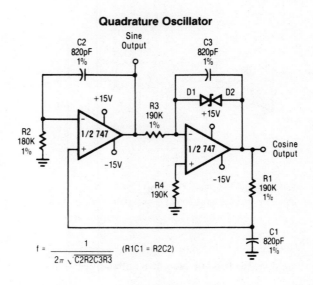

$$f = \frac{1}{2\pi \sqrt{C2R2C3R3}} \quad (R1C1 = R2C2)$$

Analog Multiplier

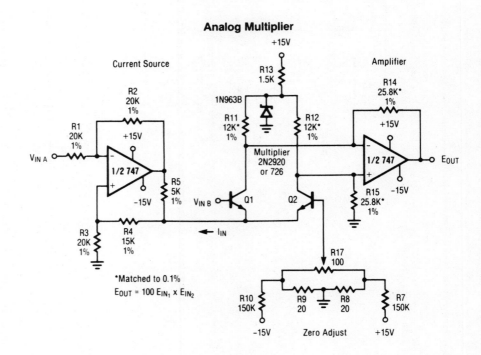

*Matched to 0.1%
$E_{OUT} = 100\ E_{IN_1} \times E_{IN_2}$

Compressor/Expander Amplifiers

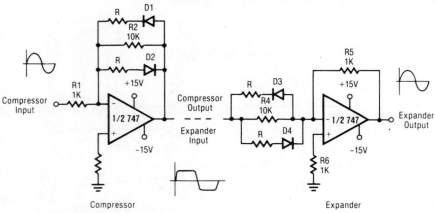

Maximum compression expansion ratio = R1/R (10KΩ > R ≥ 0)

Note: Diodes D1 through D4 are matched FD6666 or equivalent

Tracking Positive and Negative Voltage References

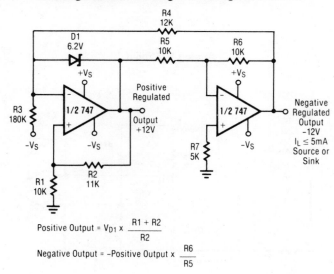

$$\text{Positive Output} = V_{D1} \times \frac{R1 + R2}{R2}$$

$$\text{Negative Output} = -\text{Positive Output} \times \frac{R6}{R5}$$

Unity Gain Voltage Follower

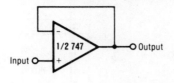

$R_{IN} = 400M\Omega$
$C_{IN} = 1pF$
$R_{OUT} \ll 1\Omega$
$BW = 1MHz$

Non-Inverting Amplifier

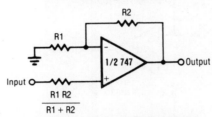

$$\frac{R1\ R2}{R1 + R2}$$

Gain	R1	R2	B.W.	R_{IN}
10	1kΩ	9kΩ	100kHz	400MΩ
100	100Ω	9.9kΩ	10kHz	280MΩ
1000	100Ω	99.9kΩ	1kHz	80MΩ

Notch Filter Using the 747 as a Gyrator

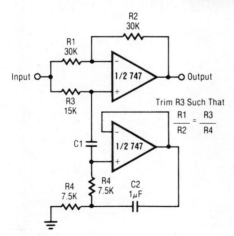

Trim R3 Such That
$$\frac{R1}{R2} = \frac{R3}{R4}$$

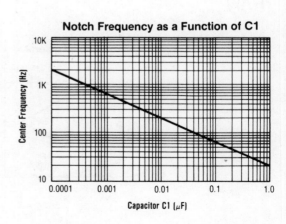

Notch Frequency as a Function of C1

Inverting Amplifier

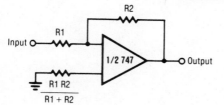

Gain	R1	R2	B.W.	R_{IN}
1	10kΩ	10kΩ	1MHz	10kΩ
10	1kΩ	10kΩ	100kHz	1kΩ
100	1kΩ	100kΩ	10kHz	1kΩ
1000	100Ω	100kΩ	1kHz	100Ω

Weighted Averaging Amplifier

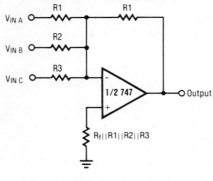

$$-V_0 = V_{IN\,A} \left(\frac{R_f}{R1} \right) - V_{IN\,B} \left(\frac{R_f}{R2} \right) - V_{IN\,C} \left(\frac{R_f}{R3} \right)$$

RC3403A, RM3503A (Ground-Sensing Quad Op Amp) *(RAY)*

Pulse Generator

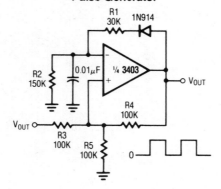

Precision Voltage-to-Frequency Converter With Isolated Output

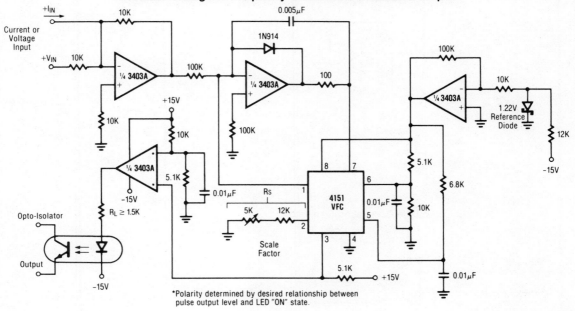

*Polarity determined by desired relationship between pulse output level and LED "ON" state.

Function Generator

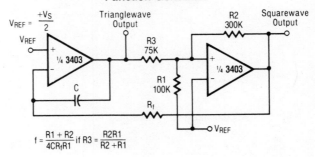

$$f = \frac{R1 + R2}{4CR_fR1} \text{ if } R3 = \frac{R2R1}{R2 + R1}$$

Ground Referencing a Differential Input Signal

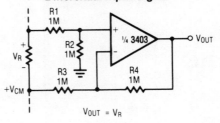

$$V_{OUT} = V_R$$

Voltage Reference

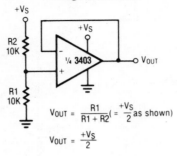

$$V_{OUT} = \frac{R1}{R1 + R2}\left(= \frac{+V_S}{2} \text{ as shown}\right)$$

$$V_{OUT} = \frac{+V_S}{2}$$

Voltage Controlled Oscillator

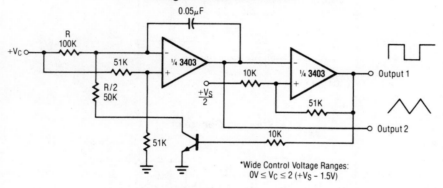

*Wide Control Voltage Ranges:
$0V \le V_C \le 2 (+V_S - 1.5V)$

AC Coupled Non-Inverting Amplifier

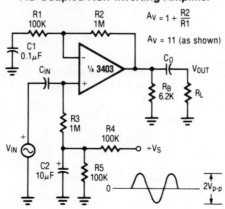

$$A_V = 1 + \frac{R2}{R1}$$

$$A_V = 11 \text{ (as shown)}$$

AC Coupled Inverting Amplifier

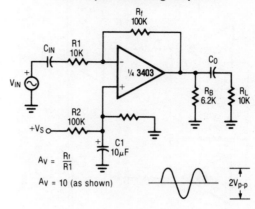

$$A_V = \frac{R_f}{R_1}$$

$A_V = 10$ (as shown)

Wein Bridge Oscillator

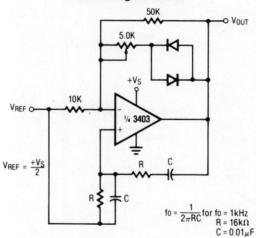

$$V_{REF} = \frac{+V_S}{2}$$

$fo = \dfrac{1}{2\pi RC}$ for fo = 1kHz
R = 16kΩ
C = 0.01μF

Multiple Feedback Bandpass Filter

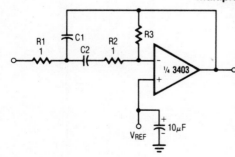

fo $\triangle$ Center Frequency
BW $\triangle$ Bandwidth
R in kΩ
C in μF

$$Q = \frac{fo}{BW} < 10$$

$$C1 = C2 = \frac{Q}{3}$$

R1 = R2 = 1 $\Big\}$ Use scaling factors in these expressions.
R3 = $9Q^2 - 1$

If source impedance is high or varies, filter may be preceeded
with voltage follower buffer to stabilize filter parameters.

Design Example:
given: Q = 5, fo = 1kHz
Let R1 = R2 = 10kΩ
then R3 = 9(5)² − 10
R3 = 215kΩ
$C = \dfrac{5}{3} = 1.6nF$

High Impedance Differential Amplifier

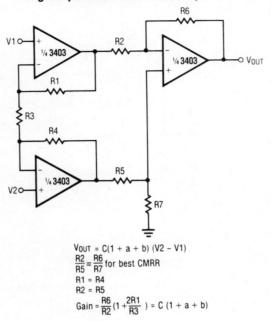

$$V_{OUT} = C(1 + a + b)(V2 - V1)$$
$$\frac{R2}{R5} \equiv \frac{R6}{R7} \text{ for best CMRR}$$
$$R1 = R4$$
$$R2 = R5$$
$$\text{Gain} = \frac{R6}{R2}\left(1 + \frac{2R1}{R3}\right) = C(1 + a + b)$$

Comparator With Hysteresis

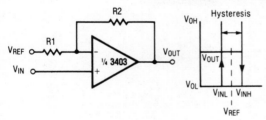

$$V_{INL} = \frac{R1}{R1 + R2}(V_{OL} - V_{REF}) + V_{REF}$$
$$V_{INH} = \frac{R1}{R1 + R2}(V_{OH} - V_{REF}) + V_{REF}$$
$$H = \frac{R1}{R1 + R2}(V_{OH} - V_{OL})$$

RC4136 (Quad 741 Op Amp) *(RAY)*

Stereo Tone Control

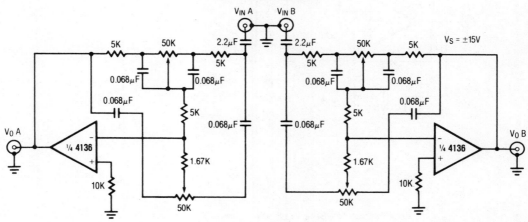

400Hz Lowpass Butterworth Active Filter

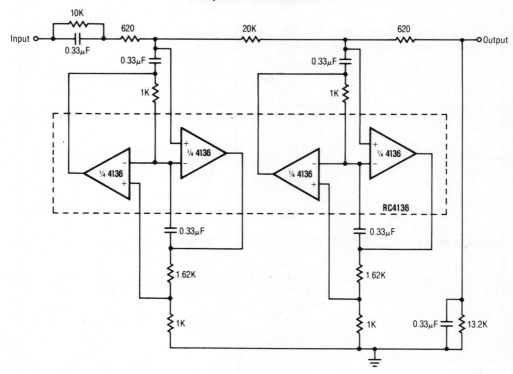

RIAA Preamplifier

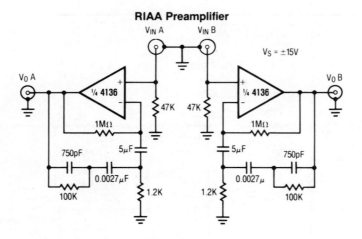

Low Frequency Sine Wave Generator
With Quadrature Output

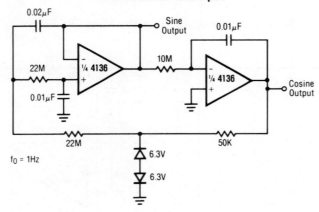

Voltage Follower

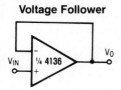

Lamp Driver

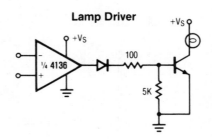

Triangular-Wave Generator

Integrator

Threshold
Detector

C1
0.1µF

Freq
140K

1.4K

¼ 4136

¼ 4136

V_{OUT}

Amp

10K

1M

8.2K

Squarewave Oscillator

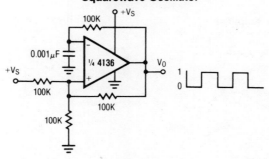

1kHz Bandpass Active Filter

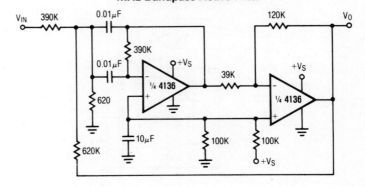

DC Coupled 1kHz Lowpass
Active Filter

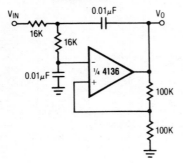

Power Amplifier

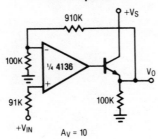

$A_V = 10$

Comparator With Hysteresis

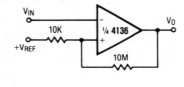

AC Coupled Non-Inverting Amplifier

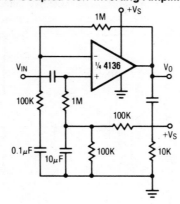

AC Coupled Inverting Amplifier

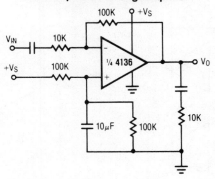

Voltage Controlled Oscillator (VCO)

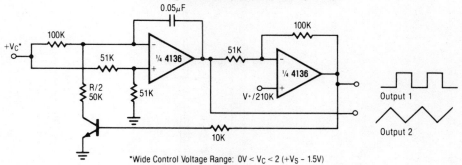

*Wide Control Voltage Range: $0V < V_C < 2 (+V_S - 1.5V)$

Full-Wave Rectifier and Averaging Filter

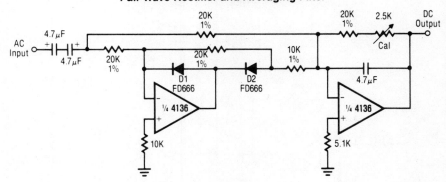

Notch Filter Using the 4136 as a Gyrator

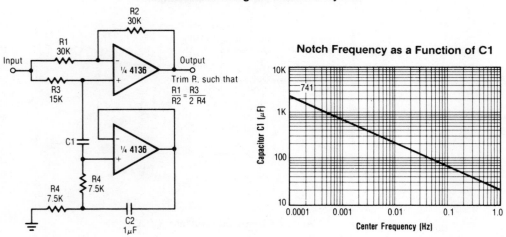

Notch Frequency as a Function of C1

Trim R. such that

$$\frac{R1}{R2} = \frac{R3}{2\ R4}$$

Analog Multiplier/Divider

$$V_0 = \frac{E1\ E2}{E3}$$

*Matched Transistors

Multiple Aperture Window Discriminator

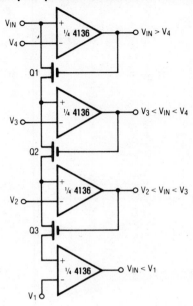

**Differential Input Instrumentation Amplifier
With High Common Mode Rejection**

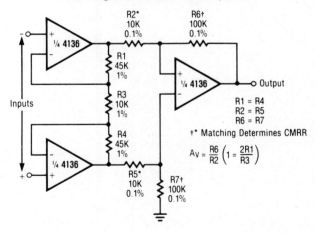

$$A_V = \frac{R6}{R2} \left(1 = \frac{2R1}{R3} \right)$$

RC4156

Triangle and Square Wave Generator

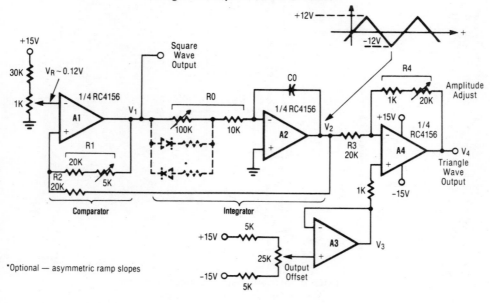

*Optional — asymmetric ramp slopes

Triangle Generator — Symmetrical Output Option

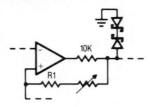

122

RC4558 (High-Gain Dual Op Amp) *(RAY)*

DC Coupled 1kHz Low-Pass Active Filter

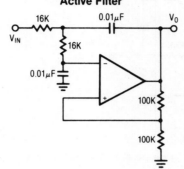

AC Coupled Inverting Amplifier

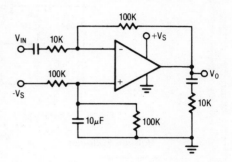

1kHz Bandpass Active Filter

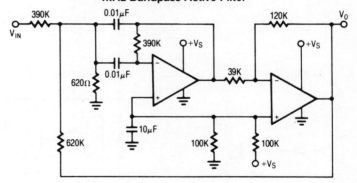

Voltage Controlled Oscillator (VCO)

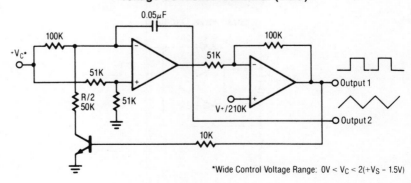

*Wide Control Voltage Range: $0V < V_C < 2(+V_S - 1.5V)$

123

AC Coupled Non-Inverting Amplifier

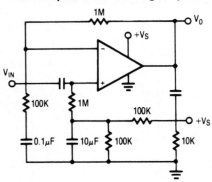

Voltage Follower

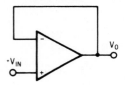

Comparator With Hysteresis

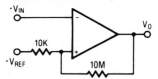

Lamp Driver

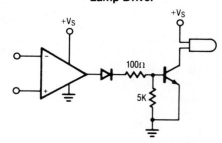

Power Amplifier

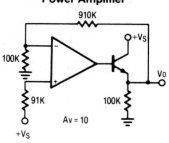

Squarewave Oscillator

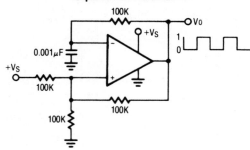

The L161 as an X100 Operational Amplifier (SIL)

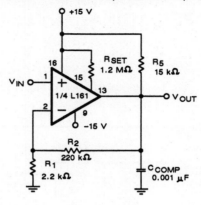

PRECISION OPERATIONAL AMPLIFIERS

Instrumentation Amplifier with 300V Common-Mode Range (LT)

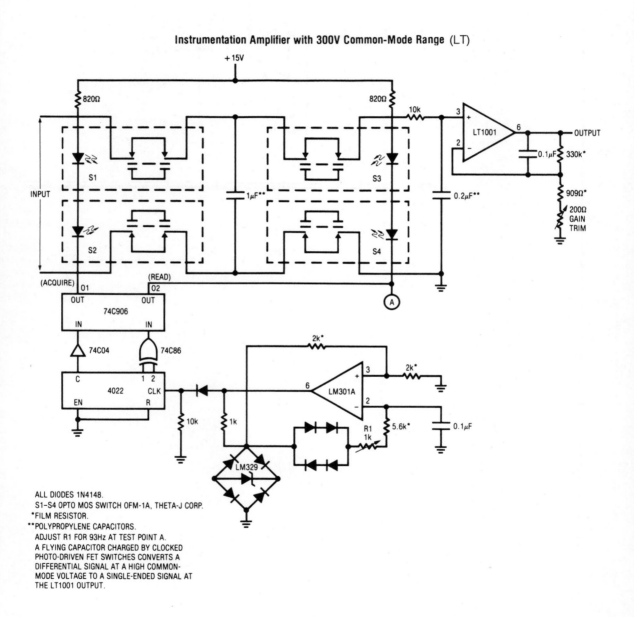

ALL DIODES 1N4148.
S1–S4 OPTO MOS SWITCH OFM-1A, THETA-J CORP.
*FILM RESISTOR.
**POLYPROPYLENE CAPACITORS.
ADJUST R1 FOR 93Hz AT TEST POINT A.
A FLYING CAPACITOR CHARGED BY CLOCKED
PHOTO-DRIVEN FET SWITCHES CONVERTS A
DIFFERENTIAL SIGNAL AT A HIGH COMMON-
MODE VOLTAGE TO A SINGLE-ENDED SIGNAL AT
THE LT1001 OUTPUT.

Linear Thermometer (LT)

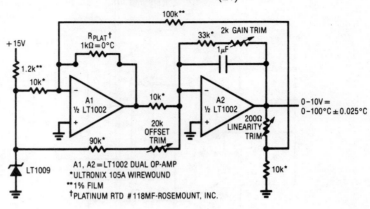

A1, A2 = LT1002 DUAL OP-AMP
*ULTRONIX 105A WIREWOUND
**1% FILM
†PLATINUM RTD #118MF-ROSEMOUNT, INC.

Ultra-Precision Variable Voltage Reference (LT)

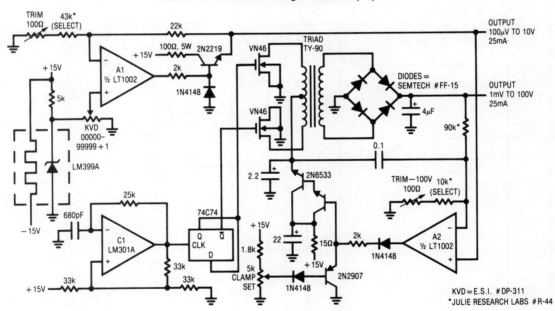

KVD = E.S.I. #DP-311
*JULIE RESEARCH LABS #R-44

Precision Adjustable Dead Zone Generator (LT)

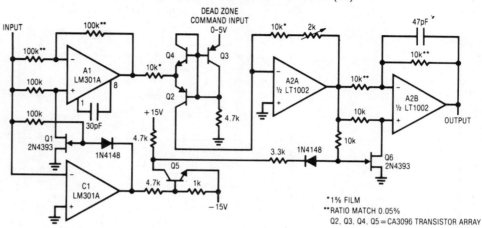

*1% FILM
**RATIO MATCH 0.05%
Q2, Q3, Q4, Q5 = CA3096 TRANSISTOR ARRAY

1000V/μs 1A Op Amp (LT)

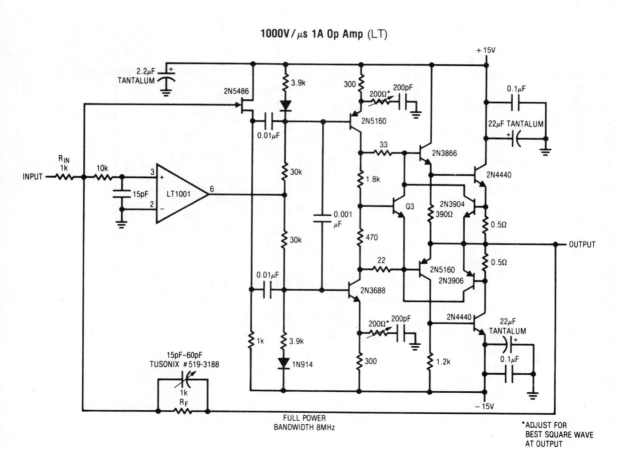

FULL POWER
BANDWIDTH 8MHz

*ADJUST FOR
BEST SQUARE WAVE
AT OUTPUT

Thermally Controlled Ni Cad Battery Charger (LT)

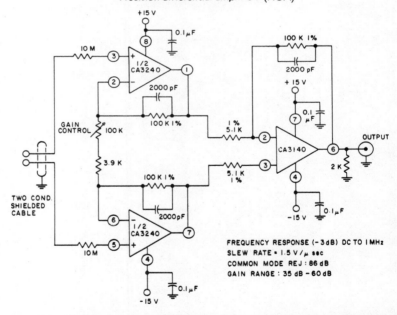

*SINGLE POINT GROUND THERMOCOUPLES ARE
†40µV/°C CHROMEL—ALUMEL (TYPE K)

Precision differential amplifier. (RCA)

FREQUENCY RESPONSE (−3dB) DC TO 1MHz
SLEW RATE = 1.5 V/µ sec
COMMON MODE REJ : 86 dB
GAIN RANGE : 35 dB − 60 dB

2

Arrays

CA3096, CA3096A, CA3096C (RCA)

Frequency comparator using CA3096E.

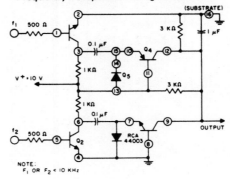

Line-operated level switch using CA3096AE or CA3096E.

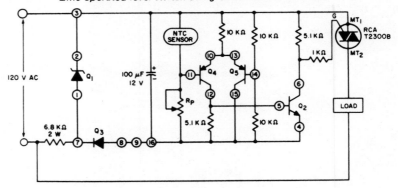

CA3096AE small-signal zero-voltage detector having noise immunity.

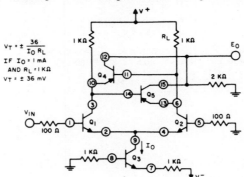

One-minute timer using CA3096AE and a MOS/FET.

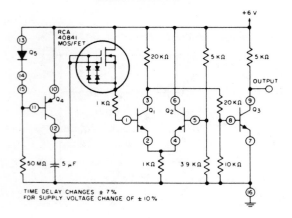

RCA
40841
MOS/FET

+6 V

20 KΩ   5 KΩ   5 KΩ

OUTPUT

1 KΩ   20 KΩ

Q5   Q4   Q1   Q2   Q3

50 MΩ   5 μF   1 KΩ   3.9 KΩ   10 KΩ

TIME DELAY CHANGES ± 7%
FOR SUPPLY VOLTAGE CHANGE OF ± 10%

CA3097 (RCA)

AC line-operated one-shot timer.

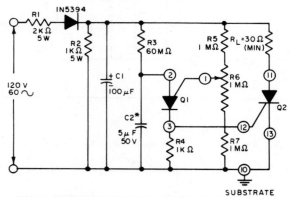

R1
2 KΩ
5 W

1N5394

R2
1 KΩ
5 W

R3
60 MΩ

R5
1 MΩ

R_L = 30 Ω
(MIN)

120 V
60 ~

+ C1
100 μF

C2*
5 μF
50 V

R4
1 KΩ

R6
1 MΩ

R7
1 MΩ

Q1   Q2

SUBSTRATE

TIMING PERIOD ≈ 200 SEC. WITH 1 MΩ POT CENTERED
TIMING CYCLE BEGINS WHEN AC IS APPLIED
* SPRAGUE TYPE 4308, 5 μF AT 50 V
SPRAGUE TYPE 6308, 5 μF AT 50 V
OR EQUIVALENT

Temperature-compensated shunt regulator.

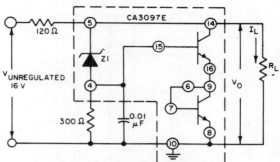

TYPICAL TEMPERATURE CHARACTERISTIC

@ $R_L = 330 \, \Omega \, \dfrac{\Delta V_O / V_O}{\Delta T} \times 100 = \pm 0.01 \% / °C$

TYP. LOAD REGULATION @ $I_L = 0$ TO 40 mA, $(\Delta V_O / V_O) \times 100 =$
-3% (NO LOAD TO FULL LOAD)

TYP. LINE REGULATION @ $R_L = 330 \, \Omega, \dfrac{\Delta V_O / V_O}{\Delta V_{UNREG.}} \times 100 = \pm 0.55 \% / V$

Pulse generator.

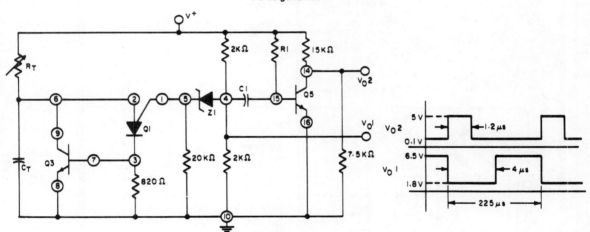

PULSE RATE ADJUSTED BY VARYING R_T OR C_T.
OUTPUT PULSE WIDTH ADJUSTED BY $R_1 C_1$
DIFFERENTIATING TIME CONSTANT

TYPICAL OPERATION FOR:
$V^+ = 15 \, V$, $C_T = 0.1 \, \mu F$, $R_T = 4.3 \, K\Omega$
$C_1 = 82 \, pF$, $R_1 = 60 \, K\Omega$

135

Monostable multivibrator with variable delay.

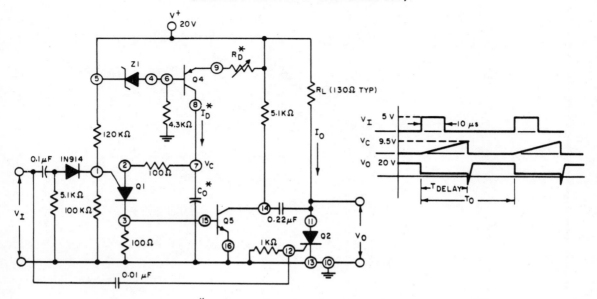

*MONOSTABLE DELAY TIME SET BY ADJUSTMENT OF I_D(VARY R_D) OR BY $C_D.I_D$ MUST BE GREATER THAN I_V OF QI (PUT) FOR MONOSTABLE OPERATION.

Q2(SCR) SWITCHING TIMES :
GATE-CONTROLLED TURN-ON TIME (t_{gt}) ≈ 50 ns (TYP)
CIRCUIT-COMMUTATED TURN-OFF TIME (t_q) ≈ IO μs (TYP)

Phase control circuit.

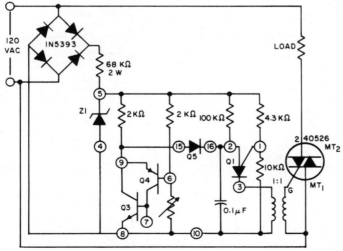

NOTE: SHORT TERMINAL 15 TO 14 WHEN USING Q5 AS A DIODE

*Low-current-drain battery-operated
long interval astable timer.*

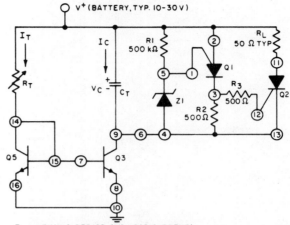

T_{OFF} = TIMING PERIOD (NO LOAD CURRENT)
PUT FIRES WHEN $V_C \approx 8\,V$

$$V_C = \frac{I_C (T_{OFF})}{C_T}, \; I_C \approx I_T \; (Q3, Q5 \text{ MATCHED})$$

I_T SET BY ADJUSTING R_T, $I_T \approx \dfrac{V^+ - 0.7}{R_T}$

T_{ON} = CAPACITOR DISCHARGE TIME THROUGH LOAD. LOAD TURNS
      OFF WHEN SCR ANODE CURRENT FALLS BELOW HOLDING
      CURRENT (I_{HO}). TYPICAL I_{HO} = 1.2 mA
EXAMPLE: FOR TIMING PERIOD OF 8.3 MIN
      C_T = 1000 μF, I_T = 16 μA
      $R_T = \dfrac{V^+ - 0.7}{I_T}$ (FOR V^+ = 16 V, $R_T \approx 1\,M\Omega$)

CA3600 *(RCA)*

± THRESHOLD DETECTOR

$$\pm \text{THRESHOLD} = \pm \text{SUPPLY} \left(\frac{R_1}{R_1 + R_2} \right)$$

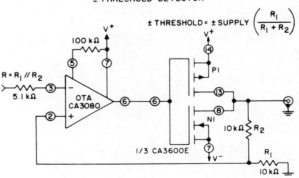

CMOS transistor-pairs used as two-stage post-amplifier to
op-amp in open-loop circuit.

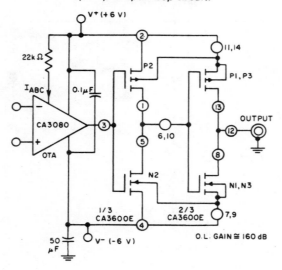

Unity-gain amplifier uses CMOS transistor-pairs as
two-stage post-amplifier to op-amp.

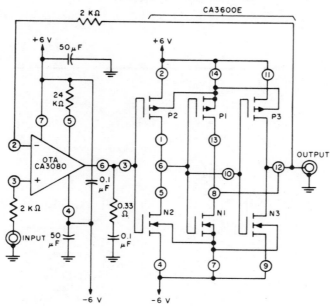

ASTABLE MULTIVIBRATOR

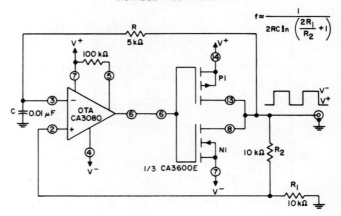

$$f \approx \frac{1}{2RC\ln\left(\frac{2R_1}{R_2}+1\right)}$$

*Alternate method of biasing CMOS transistor-pair for
linear-mode operation.*

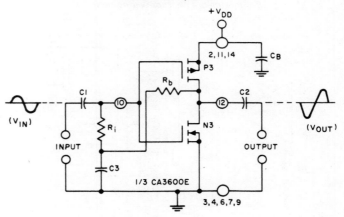

CA3600 (RCA)

MONOSTABLE MULTIVIBRATOR

$$T = RC \ln \left[\frac{\frac{R_1}{R_1 + R_2}(V^+ - V^-) + V^+ - V_D}{V^+} \right]$$

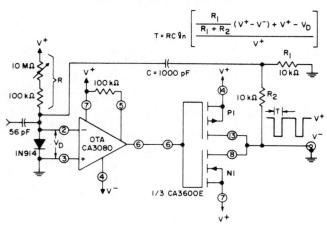

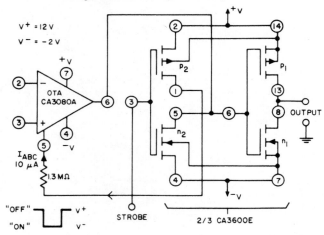

Programmable micropower comparator.

3

Comparators

1Hz–10MHz V → F Converter (LT)

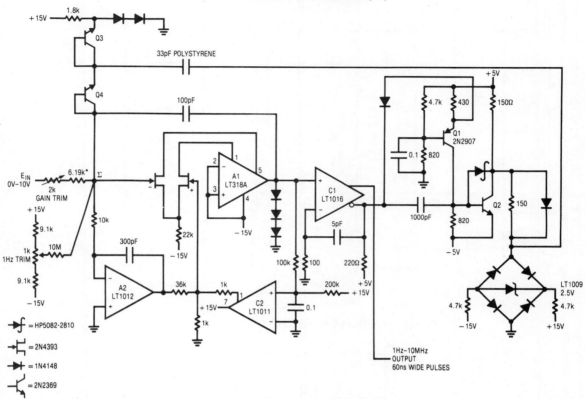

10ns Sample-and-Hold for Repetitive Signals (LT)

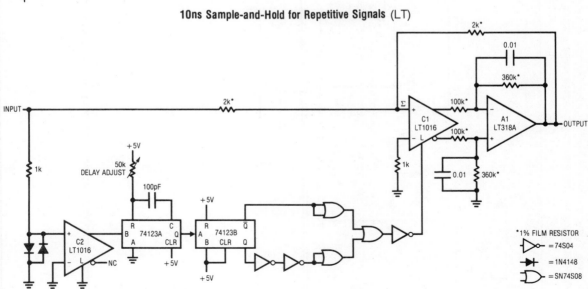

143

200 ns Sample-and-Hold (LT)

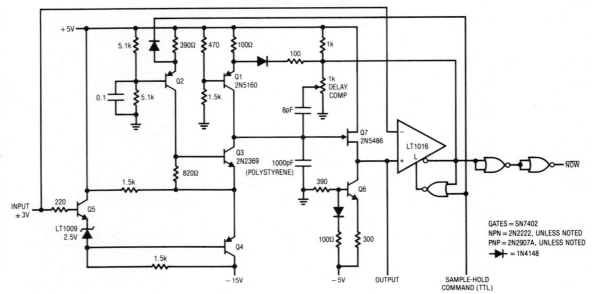

Comparator-Based Track-and-Hold (LT)

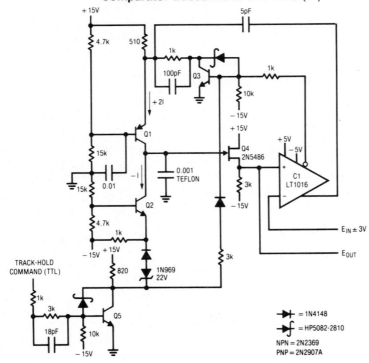

5µs, 12-Bit SAR Converter. Clock is Sped up after the Third Bit, Shortening Overall Conversion Time (LT)

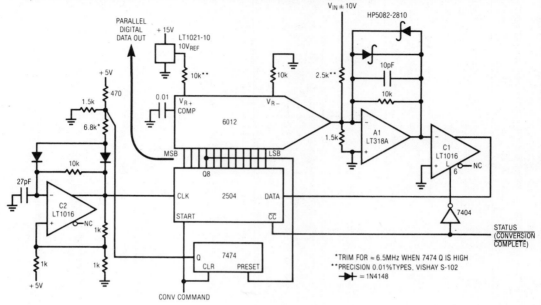

Fast Fiber Optic Receiver is Immune to Shifts in Operating Point (LT)

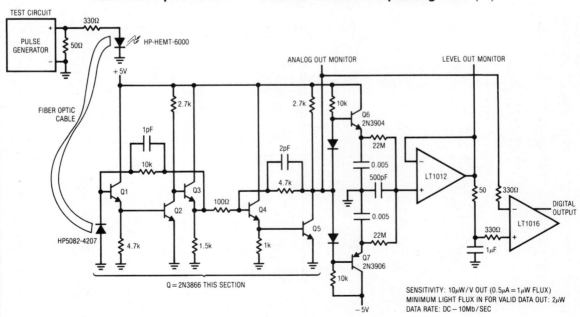

145

Fast, Synchronous Rectifier-Based AC-DC Converter (LT)

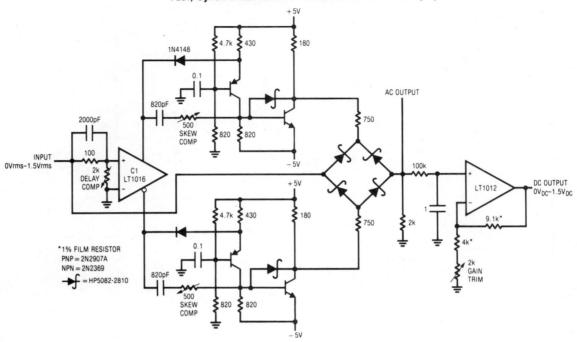

Simple, Fast 10-Bit A → D (LT)

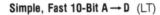

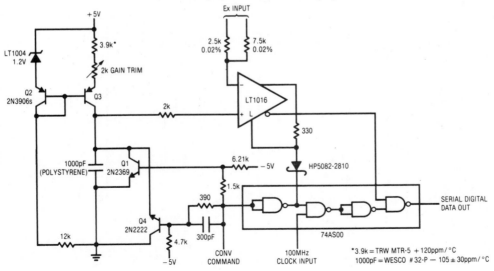

1Hz–1MHz Sine Wave Output VCO (LT)

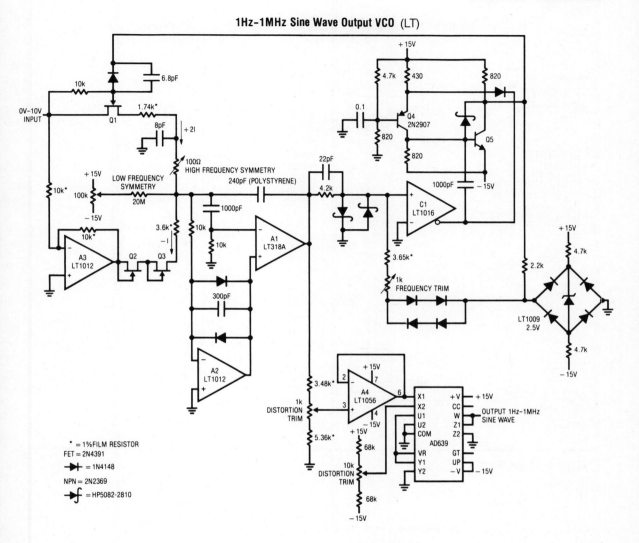

30MHz V → F Utilizes Sampled Loop for High Stability and Linearity (LT)

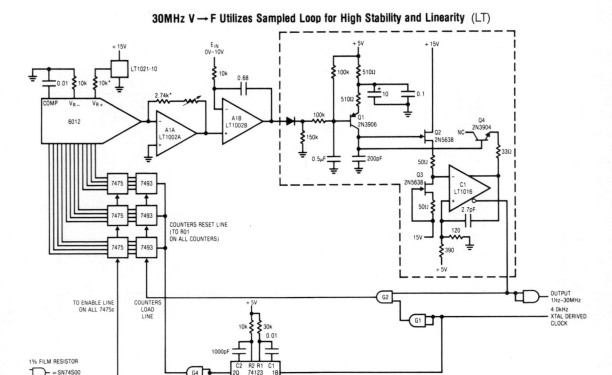

CA311, LM311 *(RCA)*

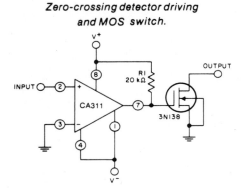

Zero-crossing detector driving and MOS switch.

· *Using clamp diodes to improve response.*

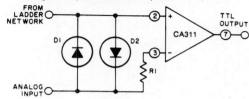

Low-voltage adjustable-reference supply.

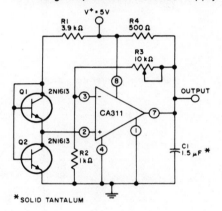

Relay driver with strobe.

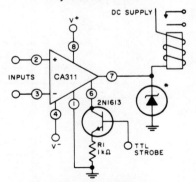

Precision photodiode comparator.

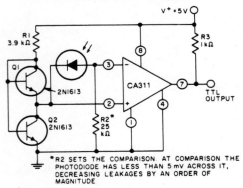

*R2 SETS THE COMPARISON. AT COMPARISON THE
PHOTODIODE HAS LESS THAN 5 mV ACROSS IT,
DECREASING LEAKAGES BY AN ORDER OF
MAGNITUDE

Switching power amplifier.

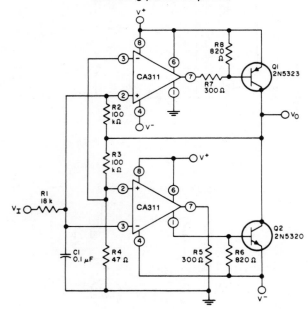

100-kHz free-running multivibrator.

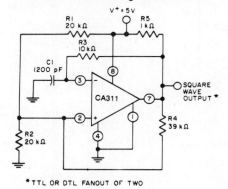

*TTL OR DTL FANOUT OF TWO

Comparator and solenoid driver.

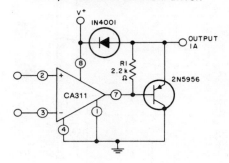

Digital transmission isolator.

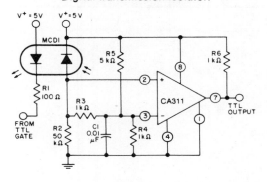

CA311, LM311, (RCA)

Driving a ground-referred load.

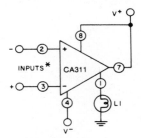

*INPUT POLARITY IS REVERSED WHEN
USING PIN I AS OUTPUT

Zero-crossing detector driving MOS logic.

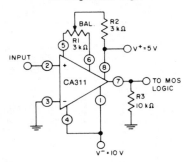

Switching power amplifier.

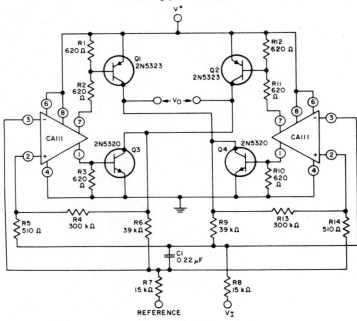

CA3098 *(RCA)*

Time delay circuit: Terminal 3 "sinks" after τ seconds.

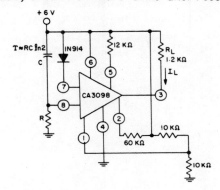

Time delay circuit: "sink" current interrupted after τ seconds.

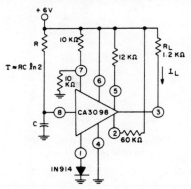

Sine-wave to square-wave converter with duty-cycle adjustment (V_1 and V_2).

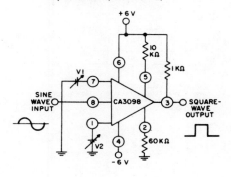

Sensitive temperature control.

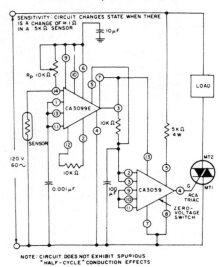

NOTE: CIRCUIT DOES NOT EXHIBIT SPURIOUS "HALF-CYCLE" CONDUCTION EFFECTS

OFF/ON control of triac with programmable hysteresis.

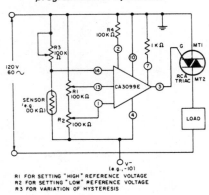

R1 FOR SETTING "HIGH" REFERENCE VOLTAGE
R2 FOR SETTING "LOW" REFERENCE VOLTAGE
R3 FOR VARIATION OF HYSTERESIS

One-shot multivibrator.

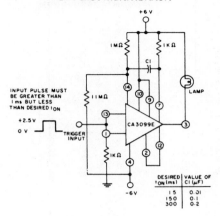

INPUT PULSE MUST
BE GREATER THAN
1 ms BUT LESS
THAN DESIRED t_{ON}

DESIRED t_{ON} (ms)	VALUE OF C1 (µF)
15	0.01
150	0.1
300	0.2

Sine-wave to square-wave converter with duty-cycle adjustment (V_1 and V_2).

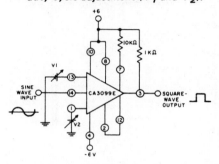

CA3290A, CA3290 *(RCA)*

Window comparator.

Both halves of the CA3290 can be used in a high input-impedance window comparator as shown in Fig. 15. The LED will be turned "on" whenever the input signal is above the lower limit (V_L) but below the upper limit (V_U), as determined by the R1/R2/R3 resistor divider.

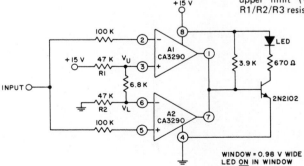

WINDOW = 0.98 V WIDE
LED ON IN WINDOW

155

Light-controlled one-shot timer.

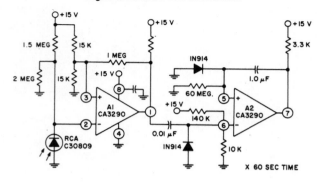

Low-frequency multivibrator.

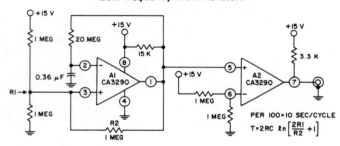

LM139/139A, 239/239A, 339/339A, LM2901, RC3302 (Single-Supply Quad Comparators) *(RAY)*

Driving TTL

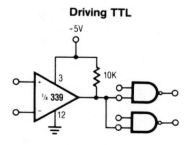

Driving CMOS

Comparator With Hysteresis

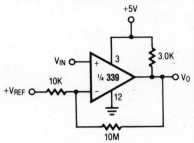

ORing the Output

Limit Comparator

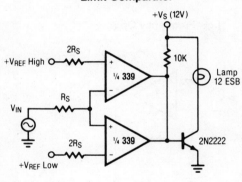

One-Shot Multivibrator With Input Lock Out

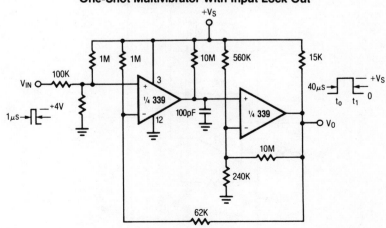

Zero Crossing Detector (Single Power Supply)

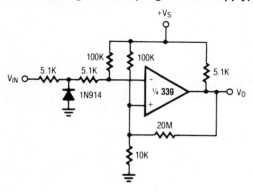

Low Frequency Op Amp

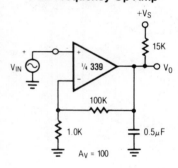

TTL to MOS Logic Converter

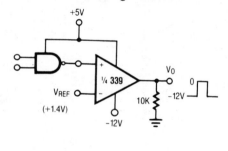

Pulse Generator

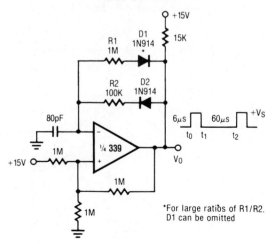

*For large ratios of R1/R2.
D1 can be omitted

RC4805 (Precision High-Speed Latching Comparator)

Successive Approximation 8, 10, or 12-bit Resolution

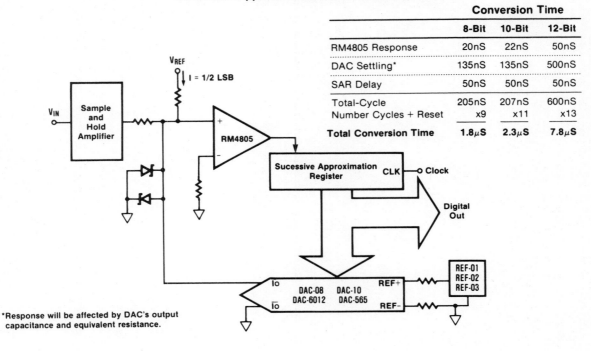

	Conversion Time		
	8-Bit	**10-Bit**	**12-Bit**
RM4805 Response	20nS	22nS	50nS
DAC Settling*	135nS	135nS	500nS
SAR Delay	50nS	50nS	50nS
Total-Cycle	205nS	207nS	600nS
Number Cycles + Reset	x9	x11	x13
Total Conversion Time	**1.8μS**	**2.3μS**	**7.8μS**

*Response will be affected by DAC's output capacitance and equivalent resistance.

Double–Ended Limit Comparator (SIL)

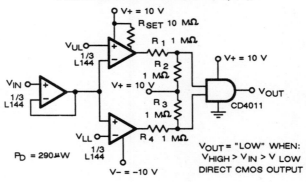

V_{OUT} = "LOW" WHEN:
$V_{HIGH} > V_{IN} > V_{LOW}$
DIRECT CMOS OUTPUT

P_D = 290μW

4

Communications

COMMUNICATIONS CIRCUITS

MC1596G/MC1496G *(MO)*

BALANCED MODULATOR-DEMODULATOR

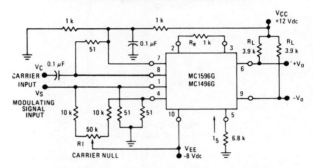

BALANCED MODULATOR
(+12 Vdc SINGLE SUPPLY)

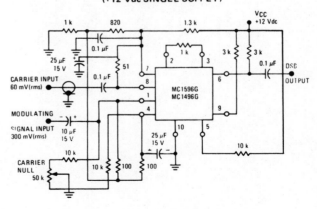

AM MODULATOR CIRCUIT

PRODUCT DETECTOR
(+12 Vdc SINGLE SUPPLY)

MC3363 (MO)

TYPICAL APPLICATION IN A PLL FREQUENCY SYNTHESIZED RECEIVER

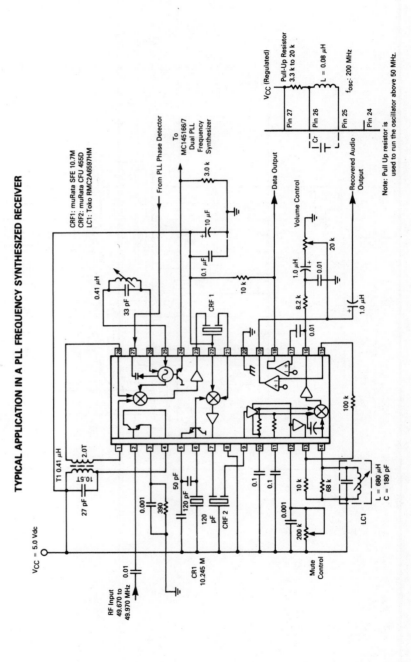

SINGLE CHANNEL CRYSTAL CONTROLLED FM RECEIVER

$V_{CC} = 5.0$ Vdc

Antenna
49.830 MHz

CRF1: muRata SFE 10.7M
CRF2: muRata CFU 455D
LC1: Toko RMC2A6597HM

1.0 k

1000 pF

20 k

1.2 μH

CR2 39.130 MHz

300

L2
0.35 μH

8T

2T

1000 pF

27 pF

0.001

390

120 pF   50 pF

CR1
10.245 M

CRF 2

CRF1

10 μF

0.1 μH

10 k

0.1

0.1

Data Output

0.001

200 k

10 k

Mute
Control

68 k

LC1

L = 680 μH
C = 180 pF

100 k

C7

0.01

8.2 k

1.0 μH

Volume Control

0.01

20 k

C10 1.0 μF

Recovered
Audio
Output

APPLICATION CIRCUIT, MANUALLY TUNED HEADPHONE RADIO (MO)

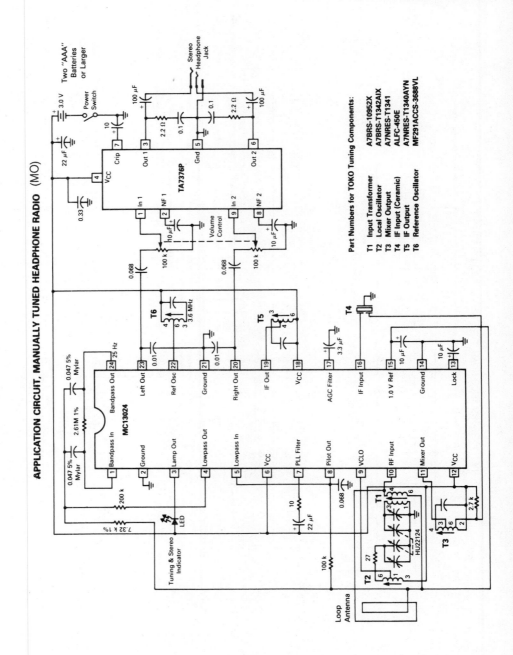

Part Numbers for TOKO Tuning Components:

T1	Input Transformer	A7BRS-10952X
T2	Local Oscillator	A7BRS-T1342AIX
T3	Mixer Output	A7NRES-T1341
T4	IF Input (Ceramic)	ALFC-450E
T5	IF Output	A7NRES-T1340AYN
T6	Reference Oscillator	MF291ACCS-3688VL

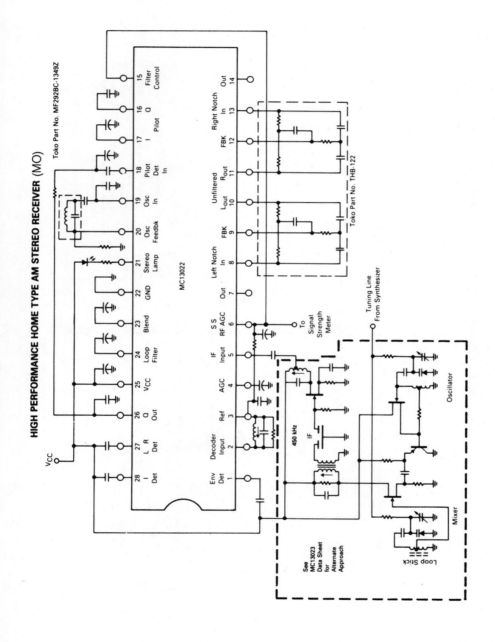

HIGH PERFORMANCE HOME TYPE AM STEREO RECEIVER (MO)

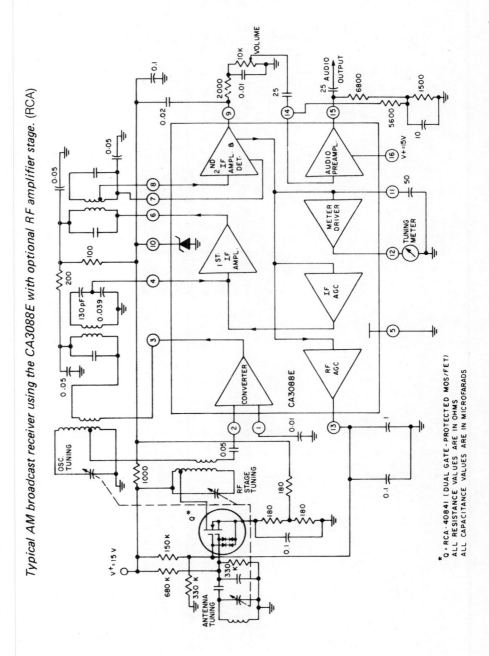

Typical AM broadcast receiver using the CA3088E with optional RF amplifier stage. (RCA)

Complete FM IF system for high-quality receivers. (MO)

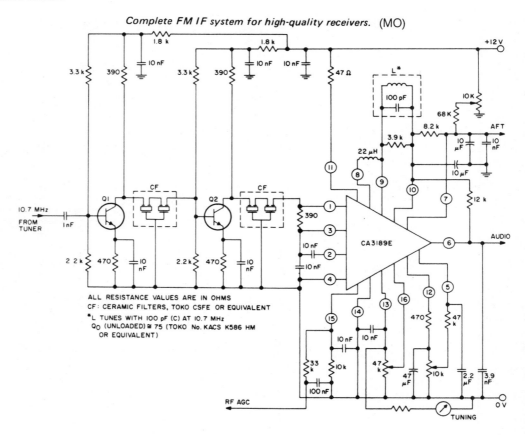

Typical FM tuner using the CA3089E with a single-tuned detector coil. (RCA)

Performance data at f_o = 98 MHz, f_{MOD} = 400 Hz,
Deviation = ±75 kHz:
- -3dB Limiting Sensitivity . . . . . 2μV (Antenna Level)
- 20dB Quieting Sensitivity . . . . . 1μV (Antenna Level)
- 30dB Quieting Sensitivity . . . . . 1.5μV (Antenna Level)

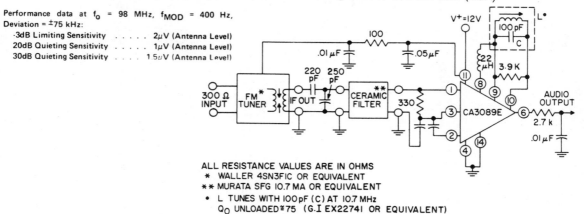

ALL RESISTANCE VALUES ARE IN OHMS
* WALLER 4SN3FlC OR EQUIVALENT
** MURATA SFG 10.7 MA OR EQUIVALENT
• L TUNES WITH 100 pF (C) AT 10.7 MHz
  Q_O UNLOADED≅75 (G.I EX22741 OR EQUIVALENT)

VIDEO/MONITOR CIRCUITS

DC test circuit.

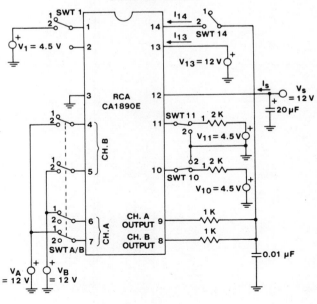

CA1890 *(RCA)*

Static test circuit.

RF Modulator

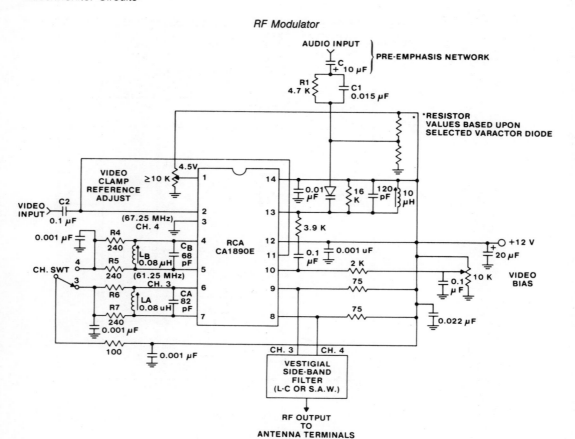

VESTIGIAL SIDE-BAND FILTER (L-C OR S.A.W.)

RF OUTPUT
TO
ANTENNA TERMINALS
OF TV RECEIVER

TV Sync/AGC/Horizontal Signal Processor

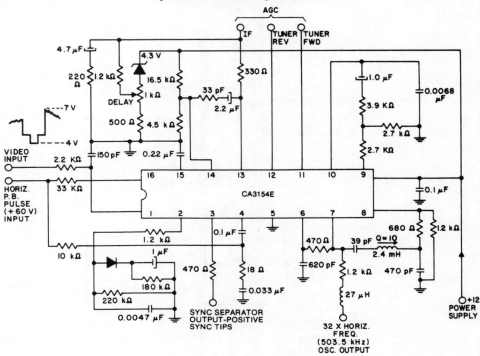

CA3210, CA3223 (RCA)

Regulator driver and pulse width modulator.

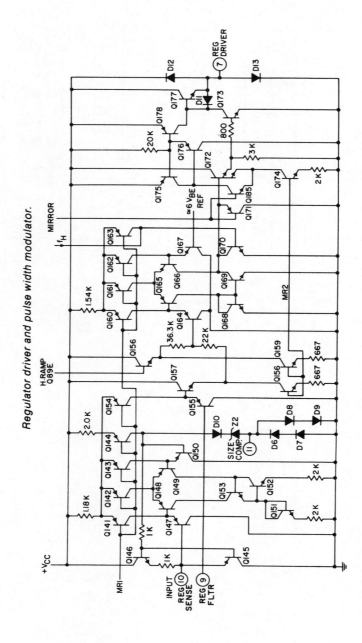

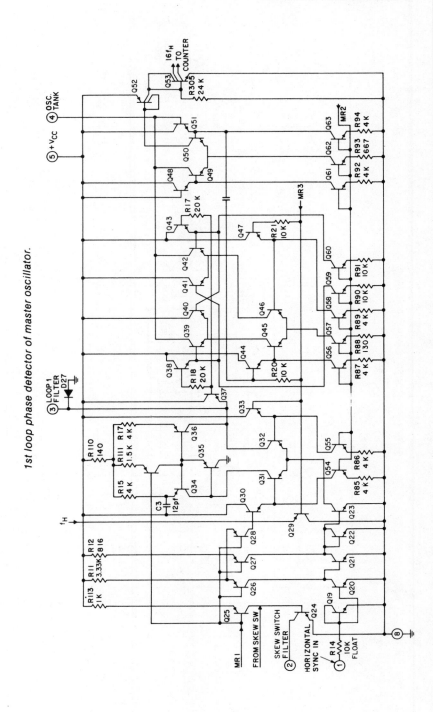

1st loop phase detector of master oscillator.

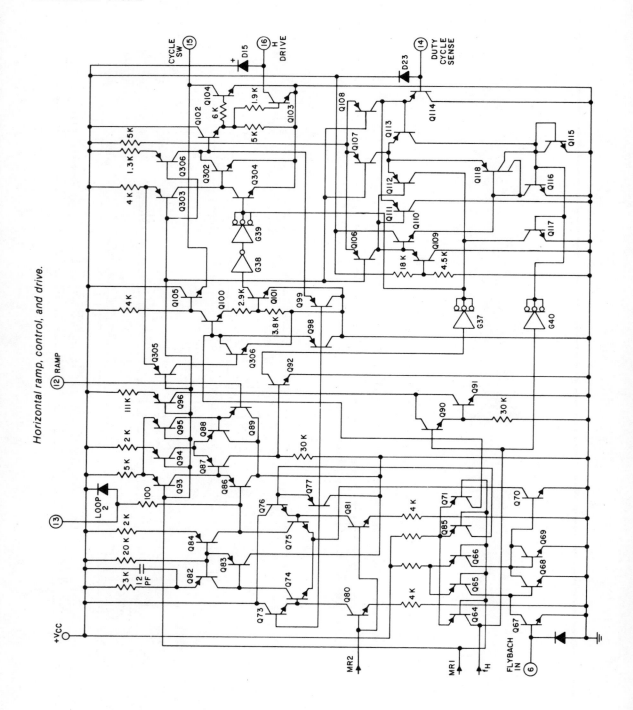

Horizontal ramp, control, and drive.

5

Miscellaneous Circuits

ARITHMETIC CIRCUITS

MC1595L/MC1495L *(MO)*

BASIC MULTIPLIER

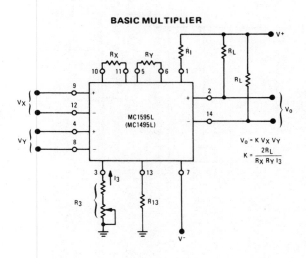

$$V_O = K\, V_X\, V_Y$$

$$K = \frac{2R_L}{R_X\, R_Y\, I_3}$$

SQUARE ROOT CIRCUIT

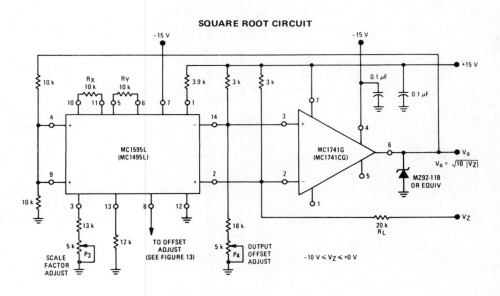

$$V_O = \sqrt{10\,|V_Z|}$$

$$-10\,V \leq V_Z \leq +0\,V$$

MULTIPLIER WITH OP-AMPL. LEVEL SHIFT

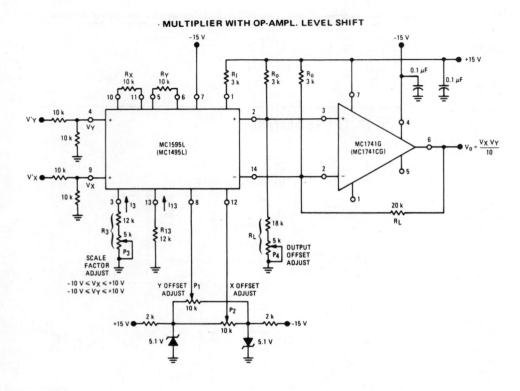

DIVIDE CIRCUIT

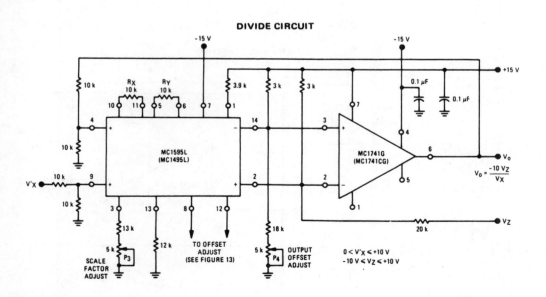

MULTIPLIER WITH IMPROVED LINEARITY

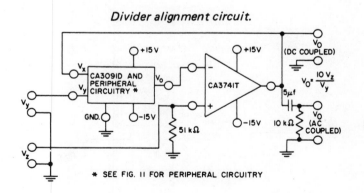

CA3091 (RCA)

Divider alignment circuit.

* SEE FIG. 11 FOR PERIPHERAL CIRCUITRY

Multifunction circuit-board arrangement with terminal connections for multiplier and squarer operation.

a) Circuit arrangement for multiplier or squarer operation.

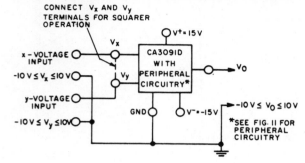

b) Terminal connections for multiplying operation.

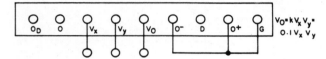

c) Terminal connections for squarer operation.

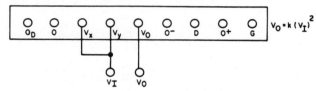

Circuit to provide offset ac signal for use in divider alignment procedure.

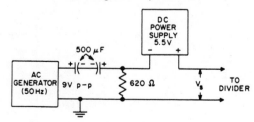

Multifunction circuit board arrangement with terminal connections for divider operation.

Circuit arrangement for divider operation.

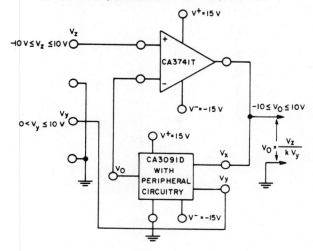

Terminal connections for divider operation.

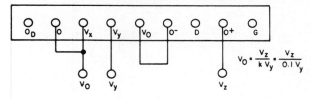

Multifunction circuit board arrangement with terminal connections for square-rooter operation.

Circuit arrangement for square-rooter operation.

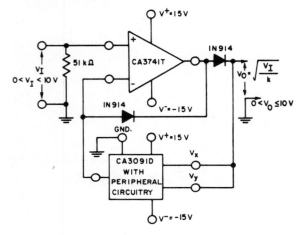

Terminal connections for square-rooter operation.

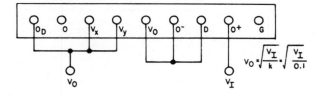

$$v_0 = \sqrt{\frac{v_I}{k}} \cdot \sqrt{\frac{v_I}{0.1}}$$

AUTOMOTIVE CIRCUITS

CA3165 *(RCA)*

Typical ignition system using the CA3165E1.

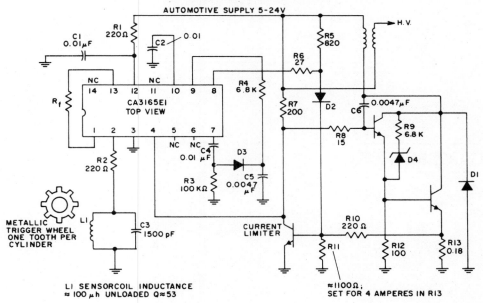

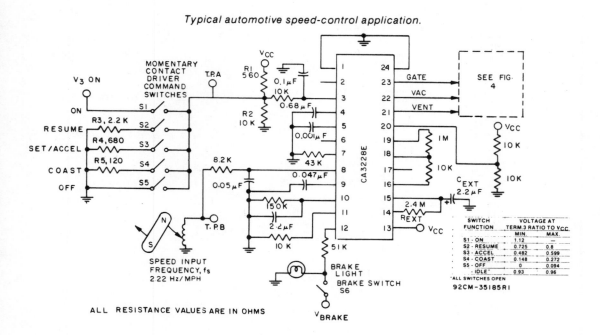

Typical ignition system using the CA3165E.

CA3228E (RCA)

Typical automotive speed-control application.

SWITCH FUNCTION	VOLTAGE AT TERM.3 RATIO TO V_{CC}	
	MIN.	MAX.
S1 - ON	1.12	—
S2 - RESUME	0.725	0.8
S3 - ACCEL	0.482	0.599
S4 - COAST	0.148	0.272
S5 - OFF	0	0.094
IDLE	0.93	0.96

*ALL SWITCHES OPEN

92CM-35185R1

Solenoid drivers and servo vacuum control mechanism typical application.

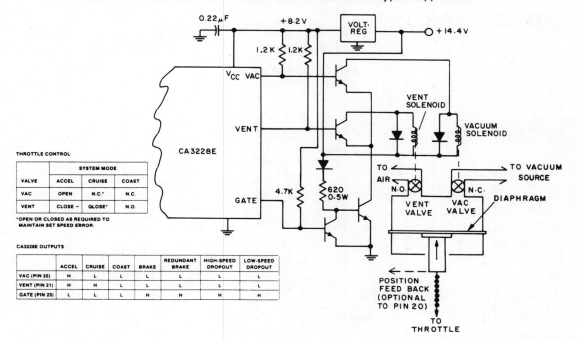

THROTTLE CONTROL

VALVE	SYSTEM MODE		
	ACCEL	CRUISE	COAST
VAC	OPEN	N.C.*	N.C.
VENT	CLOSE --	CLOSE*	N.O.

*OPEN OR CLOSED AS REQUIRED TO
MAINTAIN SET SPEED ERROR.

CA3228E OUTPUTS

	ACCEL	CRUISE	COAST	BRAKE	REDUNDANT BRAKE	HIGH-SPEED DROPOUT	LOW-SPEED DROPOUT
VAC (PIN 22)	H	L	L	L	L	L	L
VENT (PIN 21)	H	H	L	L	L	L	L
GATE (PIN 23)	L	L	L	H	H	H	H

187

DATA CONVERSION

9-BIT A/D CONVERTER (MO)

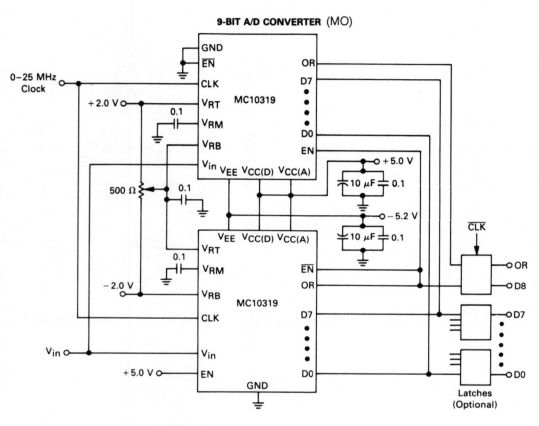

A Regulated DC to DC Converter (SIL)

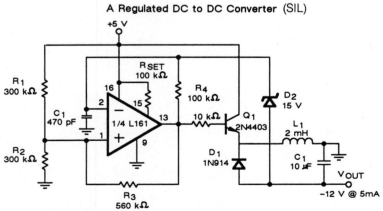

ADJUSTING V_{RM} FOR IMPROVED LINEARITY (MO)

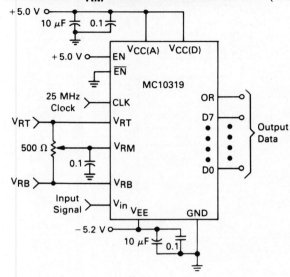

POLARITY SWITCHING CIRCUIT (MO)
(8-Bit Magnitude Plus Sign D-to-A Converter)

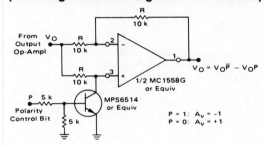

PANEL METER READOUT CIRCUIT (MO)

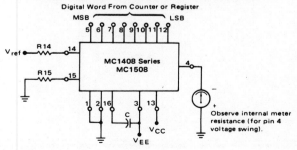

DC COUPLED DIGITAL ATTENUATOR (MO)
and DIGITAL SUBTRACTION

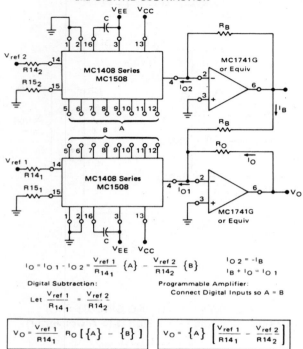

$$I_O = I_{O1} - I_{O2} = \frac{V_{ref\ 1}}{R14_1} \{A\} - \frac{V_{ref\ 2}}{R14_2} \{B\}$$

$$I_{O2} = -I_B$$
$$I_B + I_O = I_{O1}$$

Digital Subtraction:

Let $\dfrac{V_{ref\ 1}}{R14_1} = \dfrac{V_{ref\ 2}}{R14_2}$

Programmable Amplifier:
Connect Digital Inputs so A = B

$$V_O = \frac{V_{ref\ 1}}{R14_1} R_O [\{A\} - \{B\}]$$

$$V_O = \{A\} \left[\frac{V_{ref\ 1}}{R14_1} - \frac{V_{ref\ 2}}{R14_2} \right]$$

PROGRAMMABLE GAIN AMPLIFIER OR (MO)
DIGITAL ATTENUATOR CIRCUIT

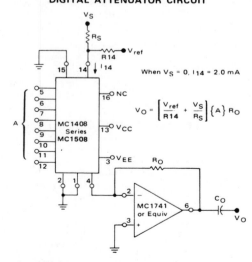

When $V_S = 0$, $I_{14} = 2.0$ mA

$$V_O = \left[\frac{V_{ref}}{R14} + \frac{V_S}{R_S} \right] \{A\} R_O$$

TEMPERATURE TRANSDUCERS *(AD)*

Differential Measurements

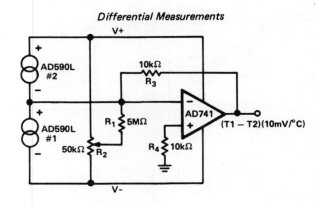

*Cold Junction Compensation Circuit for
Type J Thermocouple*

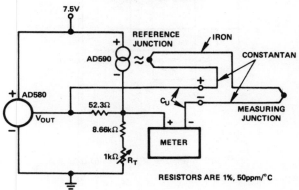

Temperature to 4–20mA Current Transmitter

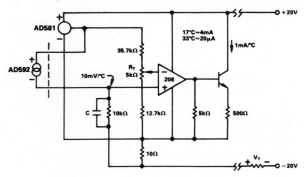

Variable Temperature Thermostat

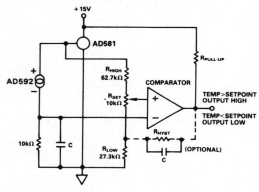

Remote Temperature Multiplexing

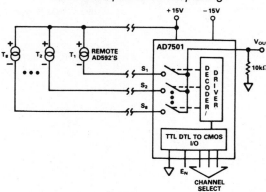

Temperature to Digital Output

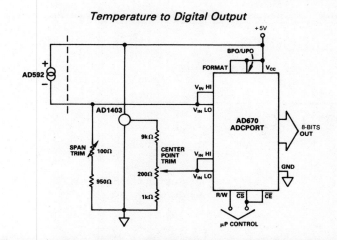

TEST CIRCUITS

CA3091D *(RCA)*

Test circuit for measurement of output
current swing capability.

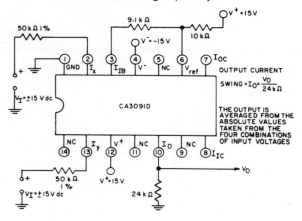

Test circuit for measurement of output
voltage swing capability.

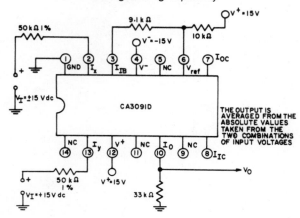

Test circuit for measurement of input resistance.

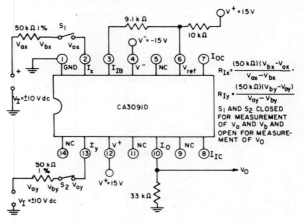

Test circuit for measurement of frequency response.

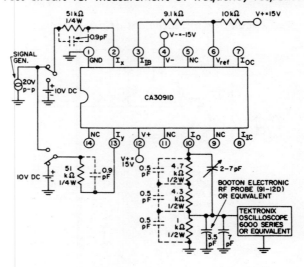

Test circuit for measurement of output resistance.

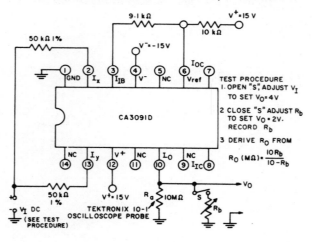

Test circuit for measurement of maximum slew rate.

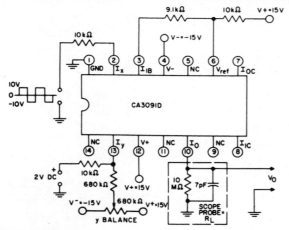

OTHER FUNCTIONS

MC3556 *(MO)*

TONE BURST GENERATOR

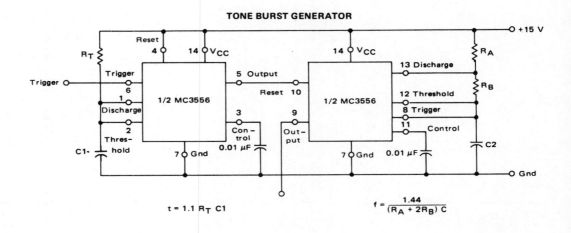

$$t = 1.1\ R_T\ C1$$

$$f = \frac{1.44}{(R_A + 2R_B)\ C}$$

DUAL ASTABLE MULTIVIBRATOR

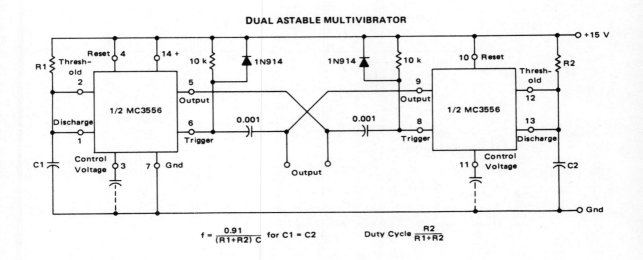

$$f = \frac{0.91}{(R1 + R2)\ C} \text{ for } C1 = C2 \qquad \text{Duty Cycle } \frac{R2}{R1 + R2}$$

LINEAR GAIN CONTROL (MO)

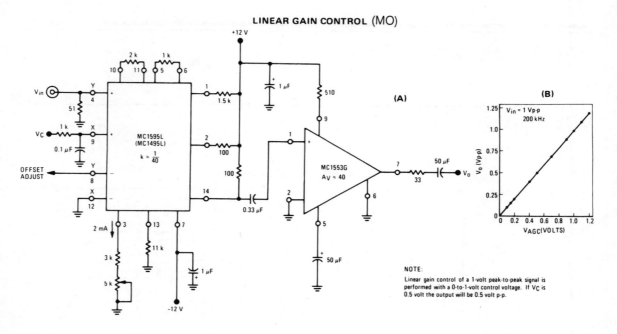

(A)

(B)

NOTE:

Linear gain control of a 1-volt peak-to-peak signal is performed with a 0-to-1-volt control voltage. If V_C is 0.5 volt the output will be 0.5 volt p-p.

CA3164A *(RCA)*

Typical photoelectric system using CA3164A.

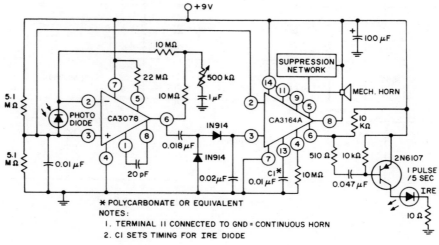

* POLYCARBONATE OR EQUIVALENT

NOTES:

1. TERMINAL 11 CONNECTED TO GND = CONTINUOUS HORN
2. CI SETS TIMING FOR IRE DIODE

Basic ionization detector with piezoelectric horn.

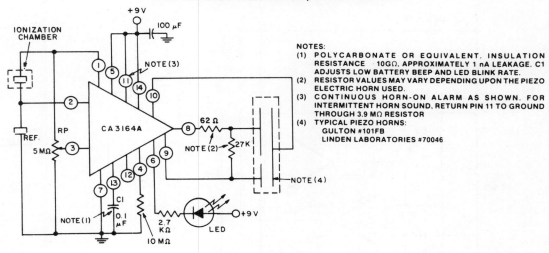

NOTES:
(1) POLYCARBONATE OR EQUIVALENT. INSULATION
     RESISTANCE   10GΩ, APPROXIMATELY 1 nA LEAKAGE. C1
     ADJUSTS LOW BATTERY BEEP AND LED BLINK RATE.
(2) RESISTOR VALUES MAY VARY DEPENDING UPON THE PIEZO
     ELECTRIC HORN USED.
(3) CONTINUOUS HORN-ON ALARM AS SHOWN. FOR
     INTERMITTENT HORN SOUND, RETURN PIN 11 TO GROUND
     THROUGH 3.9 MΩ RESISTOR
(4) TYPICAL PIEZO HORNS:
     GULTON #101FB
     LINDEN LABORATORIES #70046

L161 *(SIL)*

Low Battery Indicator

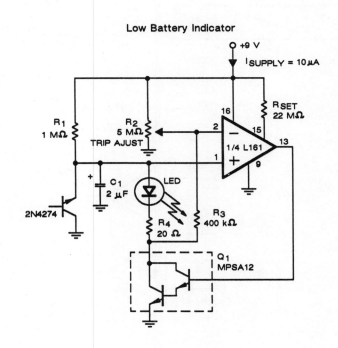

Versatile 2 φ Pulse Generator

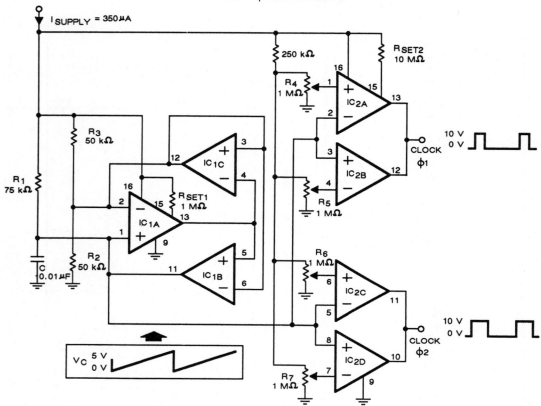

Double Ended Limit Detector

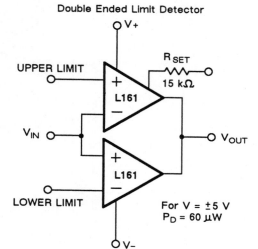

CMOS Line Receiver

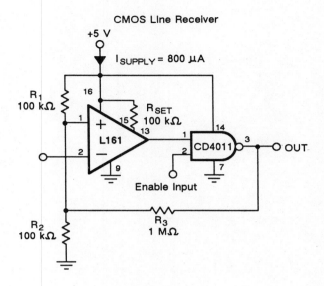

L144 (SIL)

Active Filter

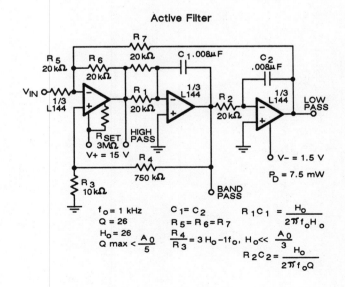

$f_o = 1$ kHz
$Q = 26$
$H_o = 26$
$Q_{max} < \dfrac{A_0}{5}$

$C_1 = C_2$
$R_5 = R_6 = R_7$
$\dfrac{R_4}{R_3} = 3H_o - 1f_o$, $H_o << \dfrac{A_0}{3}$

$R_1 C_1 = \dfrac{H_o}{2\pi f_o H_o}$

$R_2 C_2 = \dfrac{H_o}{2\pi f_o Q}$

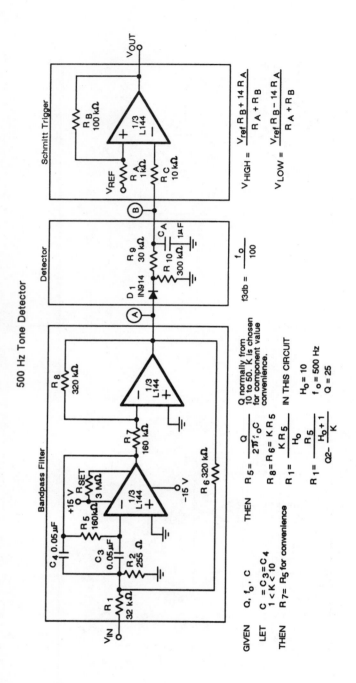

500 Hz Tone Detector

GIVEN Q, f_o, C

LET C = C_3 = C_4
1 < K < 10

THEN R_7 = R_5 for convenience

THEN R_5 = $\dfrac{Q}{2\pi f_o C}$

R_8 = R_6 = $K R_5$

R_1 = $\dfrac{H_o}{K}$ R_5

R_1 = $\dfrac{R_5}{\dfrac{H_o+1}{Q2-\dfrac{H_o+1}{K}}}$

Q normally from 10 to 50, K is chosen for component value convenience.

IN THIS CIRCUIT

H_o = 10
f_o = 500 Hz
Q = 25

6

Oscillators

Typical Gate Oscillators and the Preferred Discrete Unit (LT)

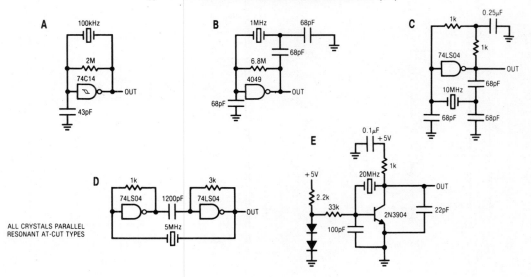

ALL CRYSTALS PARALLEL
RESONANT AT-CUT TYPES

1-10MHz Crystal Oscillator (LT)

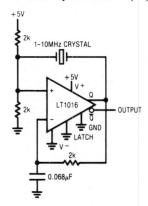

10-25MHz Crystal Oscillator (LT)

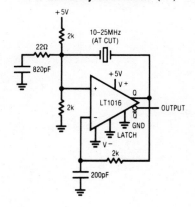

Ovenized Oscillator (LT)

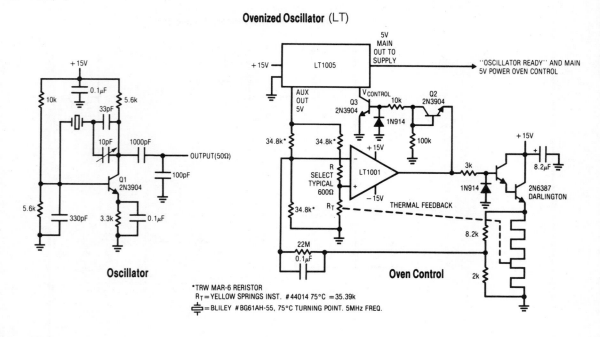

Oscillator

Oven Control

*TRW MAR-6 RERISTOR
R_T = YELLOW SPRINGS INST. #44014 75°C = 35.39k
= BLILEY #BG61AH-55, 75°C TURNING POINT. 5MHz FREQ.

LT1055 *(LT)*

Temperature Compensated Crystal Oscillator (TXCO)

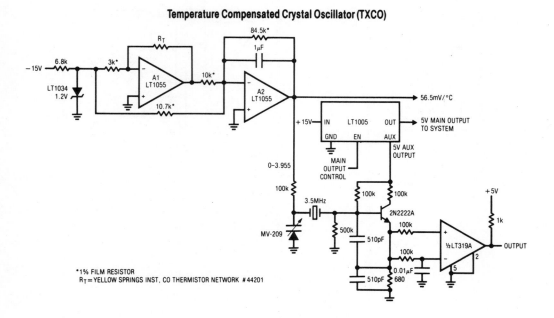

*1% FILM RESISTOR
R_T = YELLOW SPRINGS INST, CO THERMISTOR NETWORK #44201

Synchronized Oscillator

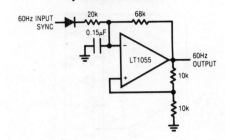

Reset Stabilized Oscillator

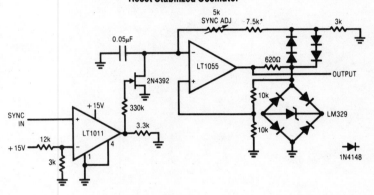

Square Wave Oscillator (LT)

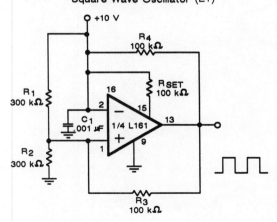

Stable RC Oscillator (SIL)

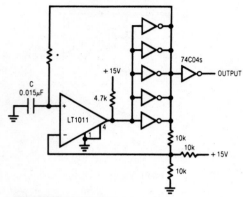

*TRW TYPE MTR-5/ + 120ppm/°C
C = 0.015μF = POLYSTYRENE —120ppm/°C ± 30ppm WESCO TYPE 32-P

7

Power
Conversion/Regulation

BATTERIES *(LT)*

Negative Voltage Generator

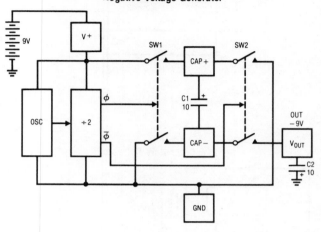

Regulated Negative Voltage Converter

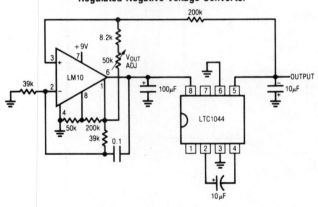

High Current Battery Splitter

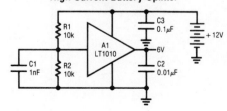

Battery Splitter

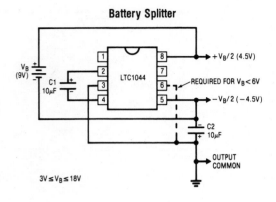

Low Dropout 5V Regulator

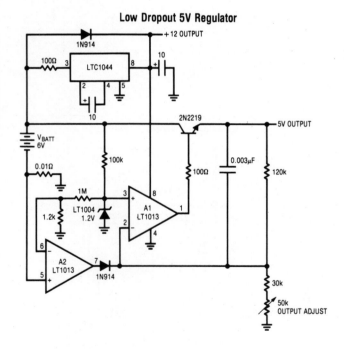

Low Power Switching Regulator

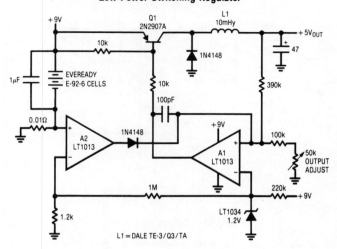

L1 = DALE TE-3/Q3/TA

"Inductorless" High Current Switching Regulator

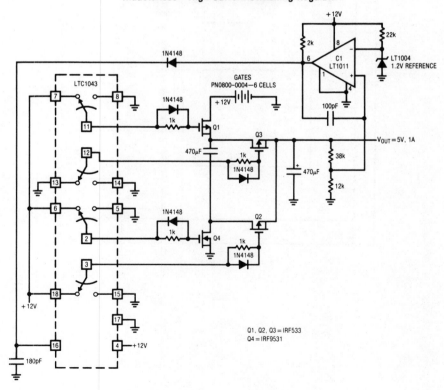

Q1, Q2, Q3 = IRF533
Q4 = IRF9531

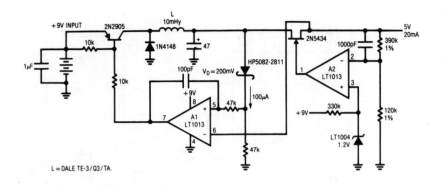

L = DALE TE-3/Q3/TA.

Regulated Voltage Up Converter

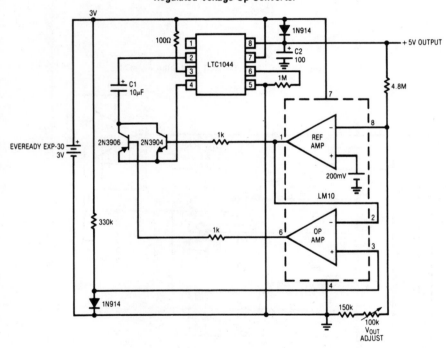

Sine Wave Output Converter

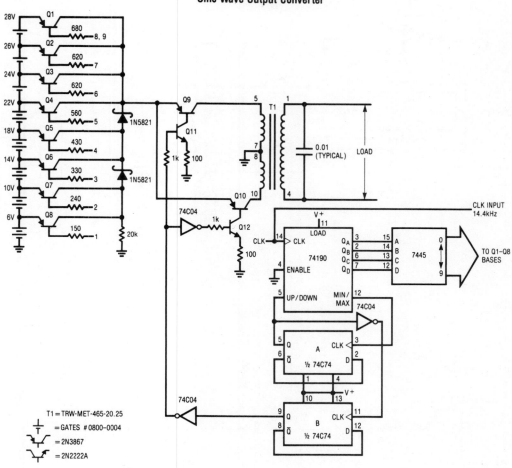

T1 = TRW-MET-465-20.25
= GATES #0800-0004
= 2N3867
= 2N2222A

Voltage Doubler

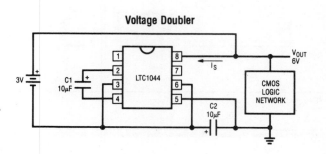

Single Inductor, Dual Polarity Regulator

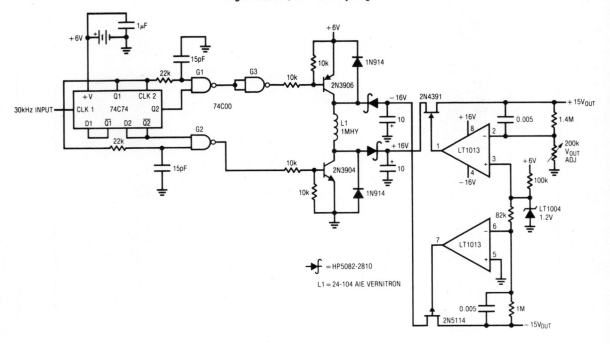

+6V-to-+15V Converter

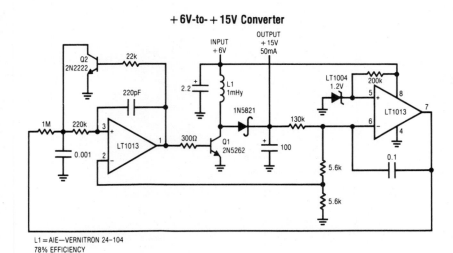

L1 = AIE—VERNITRON 24-104
78% EFFICIENCY

POWER CONTROL *(RCA)*

CA723, CA723C

Negative-voltage regulator circuit.

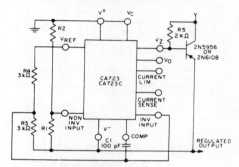

CIRCUIT PERFORMANCE DATA:
REGULATED OUTPUT VOLTAGE . . . . −15 V
LINE REGULATION (ΔV_I = 3 V) . . . . . 1 mV
LOAD REGULATION (ΔI_L = 100 mA) . . . 2 mV

Note: For applications employing the TO-5 style package
and where V_Z is required, an external 6.2-volt
zener diode should be connected in series with
V_O (Terminal 6).

*Positive-voltage-regulator circuit (with
external n-p-n pass transistor).*

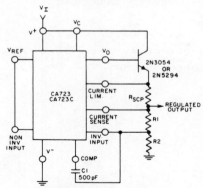

CIRCUIT PERFORMANCE DATA:
REGULATED OUTPUT VOLTAGE . . . . 15 V
LINE REGULATION (ΔV_I = 3 V) . . . . . 1.5 mV
LOAD REGULATION (ΔI_L = 1 A) . . . . . 15 mV

Positive voltage-regulator circuit (with external p-n-p pass transistor).

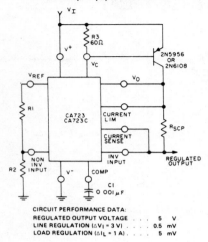

CIRCUIT PERFORMANCE DATA:
REGULATED OUTPUT VOLTAGE . . . . 5 V
LINE REGULATION (ΔV_I = 3 V) . . . . 0.5 mV
LOAD REGULATION (ΔI_L = 1 A) . . . . 5 mV

Foldback current-limiting circuit.

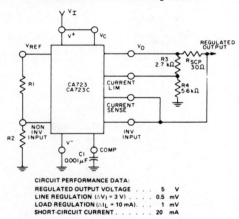

CIRCUIT PERFORMANCE DATA:
REGULATED OUTPUT VOLTAGE . . . . 5 V
LINE REGULATION (ΔV_I = 3 V) . . . . 0.5 mV
LOAD REGULATION (ΔI_L = 10 mA) . . . 1 mV
SHORT-CIRCUIT CURRENT . . . . . . 20 mA

Positive-floating regulator circuit.

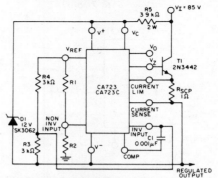

Note: For applications employing the TO-5 style
package and where V_Z is required, an external 6.2-volt zener diode should be connected in series with V_O (Terminal 6).

CIRCUIT PERFORMANCE DATA:
REGULATED OUTPUT VOLTAGE . . . . 50 V
LINE REGULATION (ΔV_I = 20 V) . . . . 15 mV
LOAD REGULATION (ΔI_L = 50 mA). . . . 20 mV

Negative-floating regulator circuit.

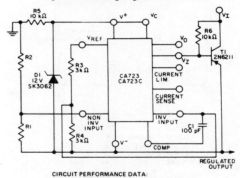

CIRCUIT PERFORMANCE DATA:
REGULATED OUTPUT VOLTAGE . . . . −100 V
LINE REGULATION (ΔV_I = 20 V) . . . 30 mV
LOAD REGULATION (ΔI_L = 100 mA) . . 20 mV

Note: For applications employing the TO-5 style
package and where V_Z is required, an external 6.2-volt zener diode should be connected in series with V_O (Terminal 6).

Low-voltage regulator circuit
(V_O = 2 to 7 volts).

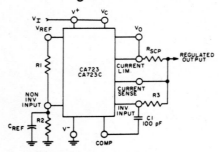

CIRCUIT PERFORMANCE DATA:

REGULATED OUTPUT VOLTAGE . . . . 5 V
LINE REGULATION (ΔV_I = 3 V) . . . . . 0.5 mV
LOAD REGULATION (ΔI_L = 50 mA). . . . 1.5 mV

Note: $R3 = \dfrac{R1\ R2}{R1+R2}$ for minimum temperature drift

High-voltage regulator circuit.
(V_O = 7 to 37 volts).

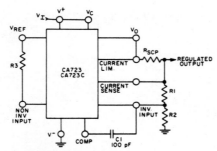

CIRCUIT PERFORMANCE DATA:

REGULATED OUTPUT VOLTAGE . . . 15 V
LINE REGULATION (ΔV_I = 3 V) . . . . . 1.5 mV
LOAD REGULATION (ΔI_L = 50 mA) . . 4.5 mV

Note: $R3 = \dfrac{R1\ R2}{R1+R2}$ for minimum temperature drift

R3 may be eliminated for minimum component count.

CA3524

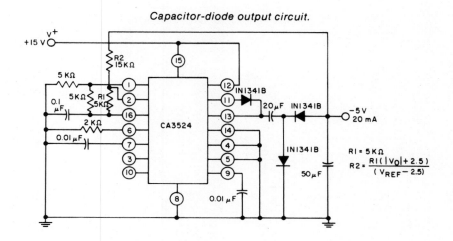

Capacitor-diode output circuit.

$$R1 = 5K\Omega$$

$$R2 = \frac{R1(|V_O| + 2.5)}{(V_{REF} - 2.5)}$$

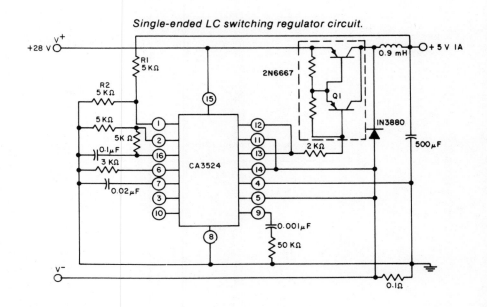

Single-ended LC switching regulator circuit.

CA3059, CA3079

Line-operated IC timer for long time periods.

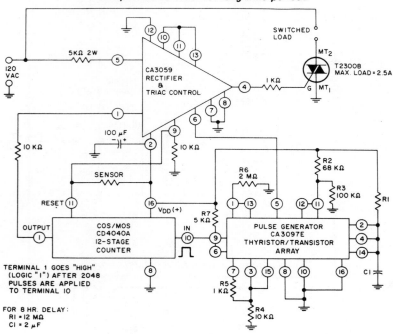

TERMINAL 1 GOES "HIGH"
(LOGIC "1") AFTER 2048
PULSES ARE APPLIED
TO TERMINAL 10

FOR 8 HR. DELAY:
RI = 12 MΩ
CI = 2 µF

Line-operated one-shot timer.

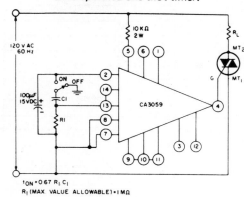

$t_{ON} = 0.67 \, R_I \, C_I$
R_I (MAX VALUE ALLOWABLE) = 1 MΩ

Line-operated thyristor control time delay turn-on circuit.

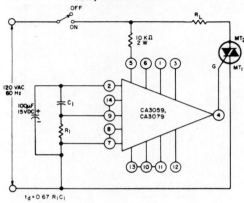

On/off temperature control circuit with delayed turn-on.

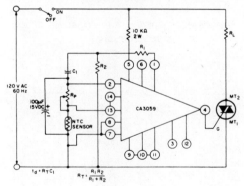

CA3085, CA3085A, CA3085B

Typical current regulator circuit.

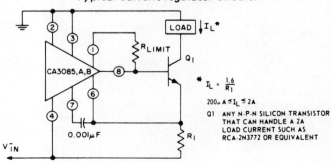

Typical high-current voltage regulator circuit.

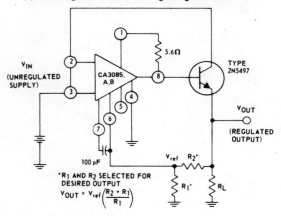

R_1 AND R_2 SELECTED FOR
DESIRED OUTPUT

$$V_{OUT} = V_{ref}\left(\frac{R_2 + R_1}{R_1}\right)$$

Combination positive and negative voltage regulator circuit.

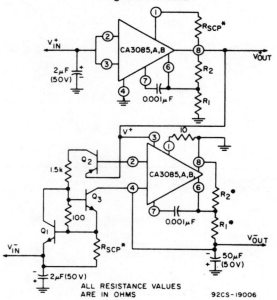

ALL RESISTANCE VALUES
ARE IN OHMS

92CS-19006

ALL RESISTANCE VALUES ARE IN OHMS

Q1 RCA-2N2102 OR EQUIVALENT
Q2 ANY P-N-P SILICON TRANSISTOR
      (RCA-2N5322 OR EQUIVALENT)
Q3 ANY N-P-N SILICON TRANSISTOR THAT CAN
      HANDLE THE DESIRED LOAD CURRENT
      (RCA-2N3772 OR EQUIVALENT)

$$\bullet V_{OUT} = \left(\frac{R_1 + R_2}{R_1}\right)$$

R_{SCP} : SHORT-CIRCUIT
PROTECTION RESISTANCE

Typical switching regulator circuit.

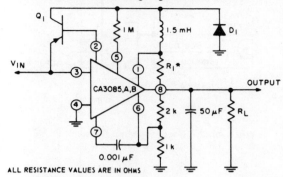

ALL RESISTANCE VALUES ARE IN OHMS

D1: RCA-1N1763A OR EQUIVALENT
Q1: RCA-2N5322 OR EQUIVALENT
*R1 = 0.7 I_L (MAX.)

CA3169

Motor driver or latching solenoid driver.

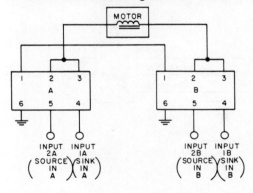

92CS-33631

When opposing inputs go low, the motor will switch direction; if source input A and sink input B both go low, current will flow from A to B. If source input B and sink input A both go low, current will flow from B to A.

225

Lamp driver.

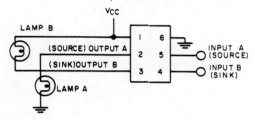

When input A goes low, lamp A will light.
When input B goes low, lamp B will light.

Non-latching solenoid.

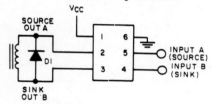

Input A and input B must both be low for the
solenoid to switch.

Relay driver.

Relay A will close when input A goes low. Relay B
will close when input B goes low. Both relays will
close when both inputs go low.

CA3242 (Quad Driver)

H-DRIVER

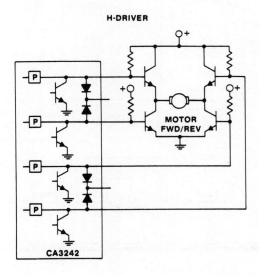

MISC. SWITCHING APPLICATIONS

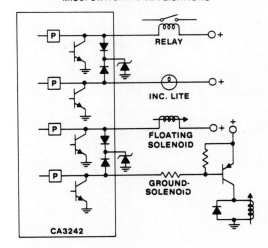

Power Control

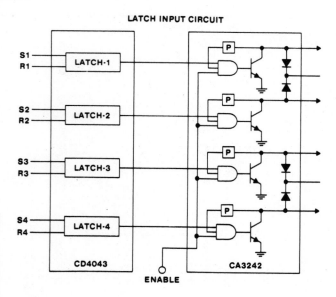

LATCH INPUT CIRCUIT

POWER/MOTOR CONTROL

MC33030 *(MO)*

SOLAR TRACKING SERVO SYSTEM

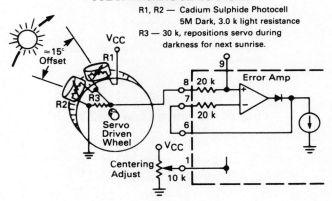

R1, R2 — Cadium Sulphide Photocell
5M Dark, 3.0 k light resistance
R3 — 30 k, repositions servo during darkness for next sunrise.

MAGNETIC SENSING SERVO SYSTEM

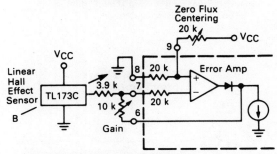

Typical sensitivity with gain set at 3.9 k
is 1.5 mV/gauss. Servo motor controls magnetic
field about sensor.

INFRARED LATCHED TWO POSITION
SERVO SYSTEM

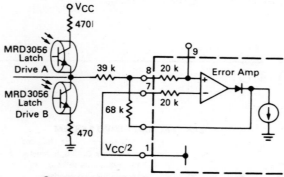

Over-current monitor (not shown) shuts down
servo when end stop is reached.

DIGITAL TWO POSITION SERVO SYSTEM

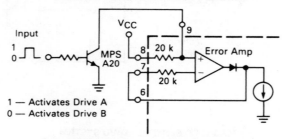

1 — Activates Drive A
0 — Activates Drive B

Over-Current monitor (not shown) shuts down
servo when end stop is reached.

0.25 Hz SQUARE-WAVE
SERVO AGITATOR

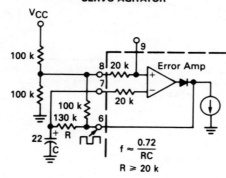

$$f \approx \frac{0.72}{RC}$$

$$R \geq 20 \text{ k}$$

SECOND ORDER LOW-PASS ACTIVE FILTER

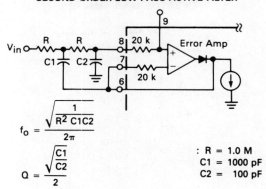

$$f_o = \frac{\sqrt{\dfrac{1}{R^2\,C1\,C2}}}{2\pi}$$

$$Q = \frac{\sqrt{\dfrac{C1}{C2}}}{2}$$

: R = 1.0 M
C1 = 1000 pF
C2 = 100 pF

NOTCH FILTER

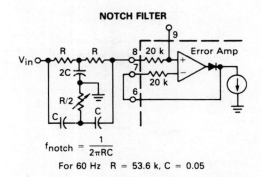

$$f_{notch} = \frac{1}{2\pi RC}$$

For 60 Hz   R = 53.6 k, C = 0.05

BRIDGE AMPLIFIER

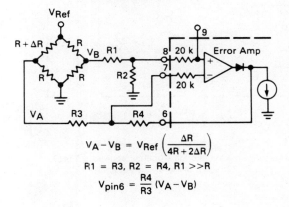

$$V_A - V_B = V_{Ref}\left(\frac{\Delta R}{4R + 2\Delta R}\right)$$

R1 = R3, R2 = R4, R1 >> R

$$V_{pin6} = \frac{R4}{R3}(V_A - V_B)$$

231

DIFFERENTIAL INPUT AMPLIFIER

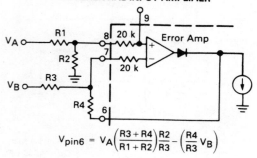

$$V_{pin6} = V_A \left(\frac{R3 + R4}{R1 + R2} \right) \frac{R2}{R3} - \left(\frac{R4}{R3} V_B \right)$$

TEMPERATURE SENSING SERVO SYSTEM

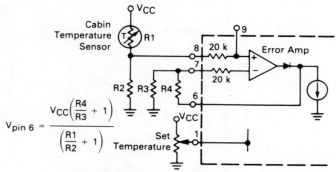

$$V_{pin\ 6} = \frac{V_{CC} \left(\frac{R4}{R3} + 1 \right)}{\left(\frac{R1}{R2} + 1 \right)}$$

In this application the servo motor drives the heat/air conditioner modulator door in a duct system.

REMOTE LATCHED SHUTDOWN

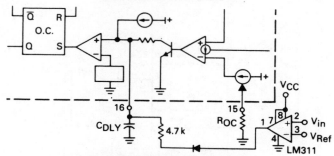

A direction change signal is required at Pins 2 or 3 to reset the over-current latch.

POWER H-SWITCH BUFFER

$$R_E \approx \frac{V_{F(D1)} + V_{F(D2)} - V_{BE(ON)}}{I_{MOTOR} - I_{DRV(max)}}$$

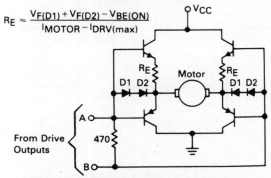

This circuit maintains the brake and over-current features of the MC33030. Set R_{OC} to 15 k for $I_{DRV(max)} \approx 0.5$ A.

SWITCHING MOTOR CONTROLLER WITH BUFFERED OUTPUT AND TACH FEEDBACK

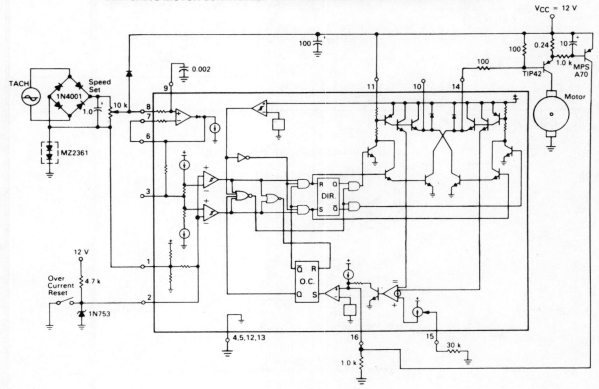

SWITCHING MOTOR CONTROLLER WITH BUFFERED OUTPUT AND BACK EMF SENSING

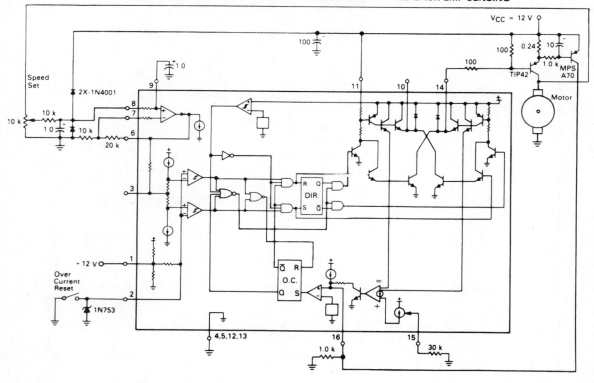

MC33034 *(MO)*

CURRENT WAVEFORM SPIKE SUPPRESSION

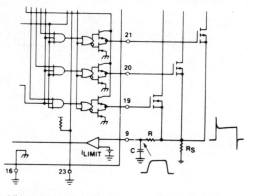

The addition of the RC filter will eliminate current-limit instability caused by the leading edge spike on the current waveform. Resistor R_S should be a low inductance type.

HIGH VOLTAGE INTERFACE WITH
NPN POWER TRANSISTORS

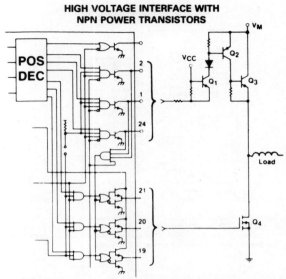

Transistor Q1 is a common base stage used to level shift from V_{CC} to the high motor voltage V_M. The collector diode is required if V_{CC} is present while V_M is low.

HIGH VOLTAGE INTERFACE WITH
'N' CHANNEL POWER MOSFETs

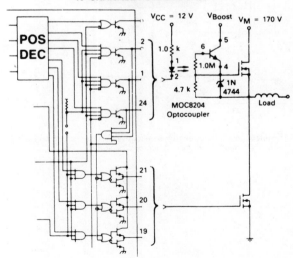

MOSFET DRIVE PRECAUTIONS

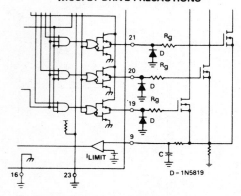

Series gate resistor R_g will damp any high frequency oscillations caused by the MOSFET input capacitance and any series wiring inductance in the gate-source circuit. Diode D is required if the negative current into the Bottom Drive Outputs exceeds 5.0 mA peak.

BIPOLAR TRANSISTOR DRIVE

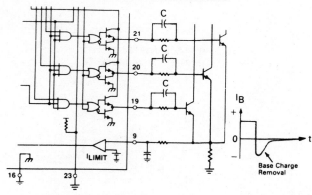

The totem-pole output can furnish negative base current for enhanced transistor turn-off, with the addition of capacitor C.

236

CURRENT SENSING POWER MOSFETs

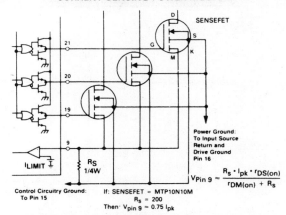

Virtually lossless current sensing can be achieved with the implementation of SENSEFET power switches.

Precision Phase Splitter (SIL)

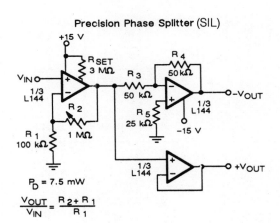

Si9100/9101

BUCK–BOOST
NON-ISOLATED 1 W SUPPLY

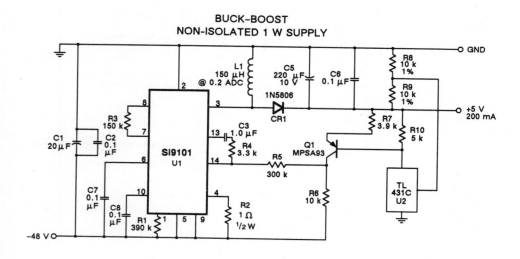

NON-ISOLATED 1 W SUPPLY (BUCK)

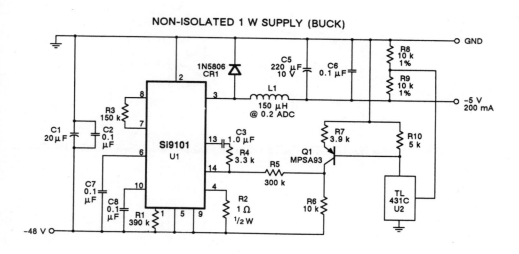

Si9102

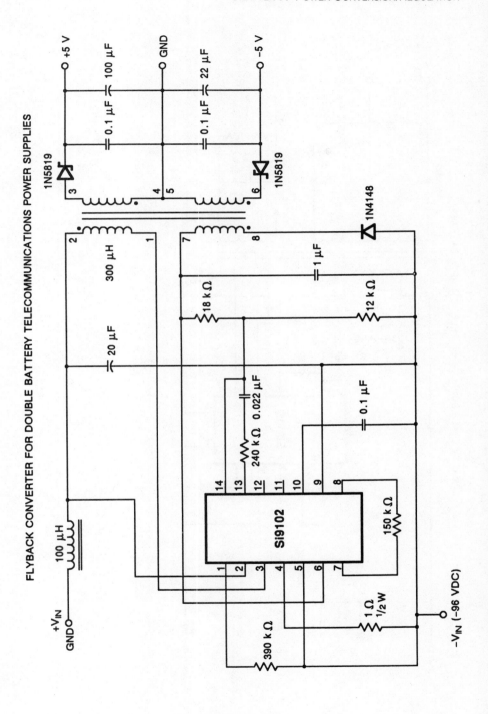

FLYBACK CONVERTER FOR DOUBLE BATTERY TELECOMMUNICATIONS POWER SUPPLIES

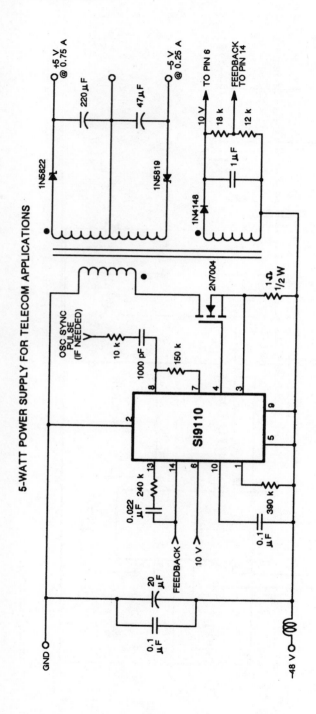

5-WATT POWER SUPPLY FOR TELECOM APPLICATIONS

POWER SUPPLIES *(MO)*

LM109, LM209, LM309

ADJUSTABLE OUTPUT REGULATOR

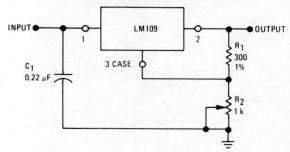

CURRENT REGULATOR

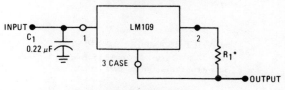

*DETERMINES OUTPUT CURRENT.

5.0-VOLT, 3.0-AMPERE REGULATOR
(with plastic boost transistor)

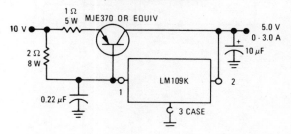

5.0 VOLT, 4.0-AMPERE TRANSISTOR
(with plastic Darlington boost transistor)

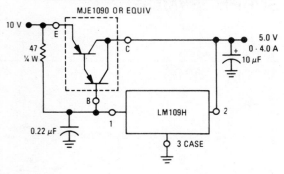

5.0-VOLT, 10-AMPERE REGULATOR

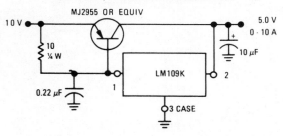

5.0-VOLT, 10-AMPERE REGULATOR
**(with Short-Circuit Current Limiting for
Safe-Area Protection of pass transistors)**

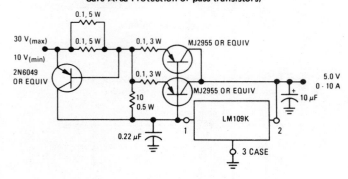

LM117

**"LABORATORY" POWER SUPPLY WITH ADJUSTABLE
CURRENT LIMIT AND OUTPUT VOLTAGE**

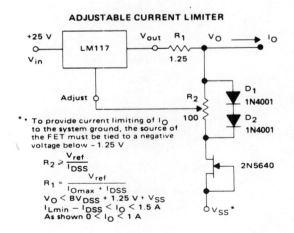

Diodes D_1 and D_2 and transistor Q_2 are added to allow adjustment
of output voltage to 0 volts.

D_6 protects both LM117's during an input short circuit.

ADJUSTABLE CURRENT LIMITER

** • To provide current limiting of I_O
to the system ground, the source of
the FET must be tied to a negative
voltage below – 1.25 V

$$R_2 \geq \frac{V_{ref}}{I_{DSS}}$$

$$R_1 = \frac{V_{ref}}{I_{Omax} + I_{DSS}}$$

$V_O < BV_{DSS} + 1.25\ V + V_{SS}$
$I_{Lmin} - I_{DSS} < I_O < 1.5\ A$
As shown $0 < I_O < 1\ A$

243

5 V ELECTRONIC SHUT DOWN REGULATOR

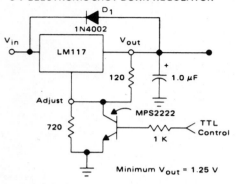

D$_1$ protects the device during an input short circuit.

CURRENT REGULATOR

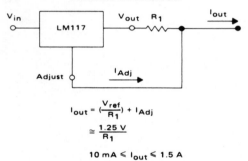

$$I_{out} = (\frac{V_{ref}}{R_1}) + I_{Adj}$$

$$\cong \frac{1.25\ V}{R_1}$$

$$10\ mA \leqslant I_{out} \leqslant 1.5\ A$$

SLOW TURN-ON REGULATOR

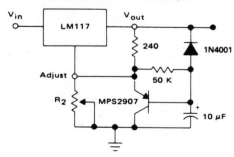

LM123

CURRENT REGULATOR

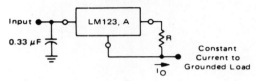

The LM123,A regulator can also be used as a current source when connected as above. Resistor R determines the current as follows:

$$I_O = \frac{5.0\text{ V}}{R} + I_B$$

$\Delta I_B \cong 0.7$ mA over line, load and temperature changes
$I_B \cong 3.5$ mA

For example, a 2-ampere current source would require R to be a 2.5 ohm, 15 W resistor and the output voltage compliance would be the input voltage less 7.5 volts.

ADJUSTABLE OUTPUT REGULATOR

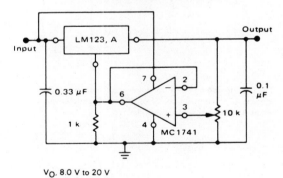

V_O. 8.0 V to 20 V
$V_{in} - V_O \geqslant 2.5$ V

The addition of an operational amplifier allows adjustment to higher or intermediate values while retaining regulation characteristics. The minimum voltage obtainable with this arrangement is 3.0 volts greater than the regulator voltage.

CURRENT BOOST REGULATOR

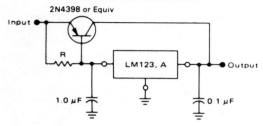

The LM123,A series can be current boosted with a PNP transistor. The 2N4398 provides current to 15 amperes. Resistor R in conjunction with the V_{BE} of the PNP determines when the pass transistor begins conducting; this circuit is not short-circuit proof. Input-output differential voltage minimum is increased by the V_{BE} of the pass transistor.

CURRENT BOOST WITH
SHORT-CIRCUIT PROTECTION

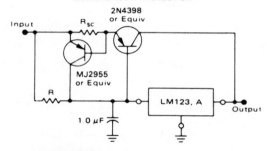

The current sensing PNP must be able to handle the short-circuit current of the three-terminal regulator. Therefore, an eight-ampere power transistor is specified.

MC1466

A 0-TO-250 VOLT, 0.1-AMPERE REGULATOR

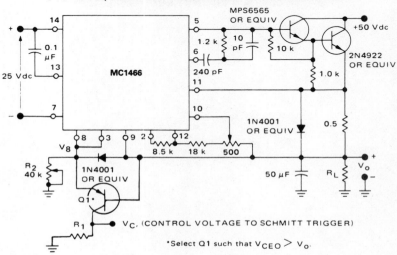

0-TO--40 Vdc, 0.5-AMPERE REGULATOR WITH MODE INDICATOR

*Select Q1 such that $V_{CEO} > V_o$.

LM2931 Series

5.0 A LOW DIFFERENTIAL VOLTAGE REGULATOR

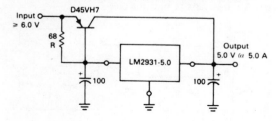

CURRENT BOOST REGULATOR WITH
SHORT-CIRCUIT PROJECTION

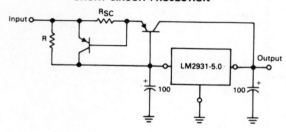

CONSTANT INTENSITY LAMP FLASHER

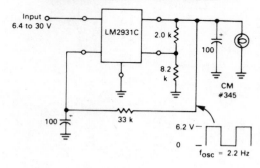

MC1568/MC1468

BASIC 50-mA REGULATOR

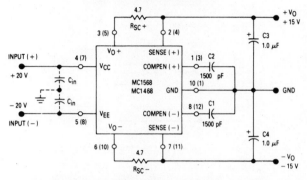

C1 and C2 should be located as close to the device as possible. A 0.1 μF ceramic capacitor (C_{in}) may be required on the input lines if the device is located an appreciable distance from the rectifier filter capacitors. C3 and C4 may be increased to improve load transient response and to reduce the output noise voltage. At low temperature operation, it may be necessary to bypass C4 with a 0.1 μF ceramic disc capacitor.

± 1.5-AMPERE REGULATOR
(Short-Circuit Protected, with Proper Heatsinking)

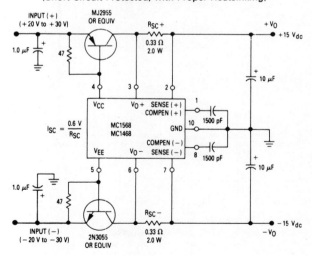

VOLTAGE ADJUST AND
BALANCE ADJUST CIRCUIT

(14.5 V ≤ V_{out} ≤ 20 V)

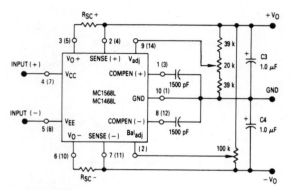

Balance adjust available in MC1568L, MC1468L ceramic dual in-line package only.

OUTPUT VOLTAGE ADJUSTMENT
FOR 8.0 V ≤ |±V_O| ≤ 14.5 V
(Ceramic-Packaged Devices Only)

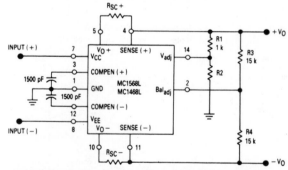

The presence of Bal$_{adj}$, pin 2, on devices housed in the dual in-line package (L suffix) allows the user to adjust the output voltages down to ±8.0 V. The required value of resistor R2 can be calculated from

$$R2 = \frac{R1 \; R_{int} \; (\phi + V_z)}{R_{int} \; (V_O - \phi - V_z) - \phi R1}$$

Where: R_{int} = An Internal Resistor = R1 = 1.0 kΩ
ϕ = 0.68 V
V_z = 6.6 V

Some common design values are listed below:

±V_O(V)	R2	T_C V_O (%/°C)	I_B + (mA)
14	1.2 k	0.003	10
12	1.8 k	0.022	7.2
10	3.5 k	0.025	5.0
8.0	∞	0.028	2.6

MC1723

Pin numbers adjacent to terminals are for the metal package;
pin numbers in parenthesis are for the dual in-line packages.

TYPICAL CONNECTION FOR $2 < V_O < 7$

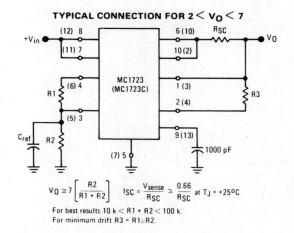

$$V_O \cong 7\left[\frac{R2}{R1+R2}\right] \qquad I_{SC} = \frac{V_{sense}}{R_{SC}} \cong \frac{0.66}{R_{SC}} \text{ at } T_J = +25°C$$

For best results $10\text{ k} < R1 + R2 < 100\text{ k}$.
For minimum drift $R3 = R1 \| R2$.

MC1723,C FOLDBACK CONNECTION

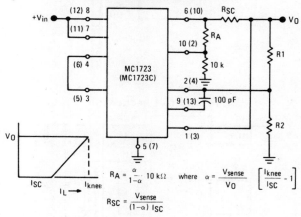

$$R_A = \frac{\alpha}{1-\alpha}\, 10\text{ k}\Omega \qquad \text{where} \qquad \alpha = \frac{V_{sense}}{V_O}\left[\frac{I_{knee}}{I_{SC}} - 1\right]$$

$$R_{SC} = \frac{V_{sense}}{(1-\alpha)\, I_{SC}}$$

+5 V, 1-AMPERE SWITCHING REGULATOR

2N4918 or Equiv

1 mH

1N4001
or Equiv

(11) 7

(12) 8

100

(6) 4

V$_{in}$
+10 V

6 (10)

10

V$_0$
+5 V

MC1723
(MC1723C)

10(2)

2.2 k

1 M

1 (3)

2 (4)

100 µF

+
−

1 k

0.1 µF

5.1 k

(5) 3

5 (7)

+5 V, 1-AMPERE HIGH
EFFICIENCY REGULATOR

V$_{in}$ 1
+6.5 V

0.1 µF

2N3055
or Equiv

0.33

V$_0$
+5 V

V$_{in}$ 2
+10 V

(12) 8

6 (10)

(11) 7

10 (2)

(6) 4

MC1723
(MC1723C)

1 (3)

2 k

2 (4)

(5) 3

9 (13)

5.1 k

(7) 5

1000 pF

–15 V NEGATIVE REGULATOR

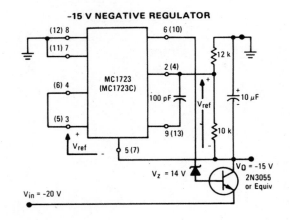

(12) 8

6 (10)

(11) 7

12 k

2 (4)

MC1723
(MC1723C)

100 µF

+
−

10 µF

(6) 4

V$_{ref}$

(5) 3

9 (13)

+

10 k

V$_{ref}$

5 (7)

V$_0$ = –15 V

V$_z$ = 14 V

2N3055
or Equiv

V$_{in}$ = –20 V

**+15 V, 1-AMPERE REGULATOR
WITH REMOTE SENSE**

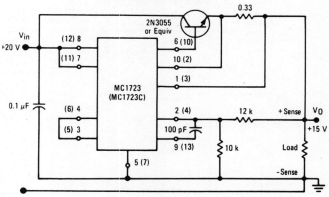

MC3245

**OVERVOLTAGE PROTECTION AND
UNDER VOLTAGE FAULT INDICATION WITH
PROGRAMMABLE DELAY**

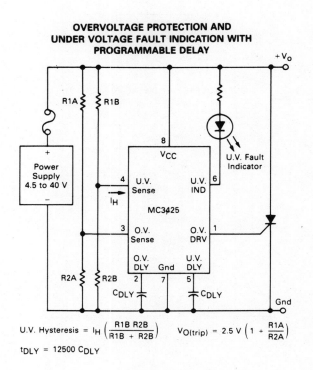

$$\text{U.V. Hysteresis} = I_H \left(\frac{R1B\ R2B}{R1B + R2B} \right) \qquad V_{O(trip)} = 2.5\ V \left(1 + \frac{R1A}{R2A} \right)$$

$$t_{DLY} = 12500\ C_{DLY}$$

253

OVERVOLTAGE PROTECTION OF 5.0 V
SUPPLY WITH LINE LOSS DETECTOR

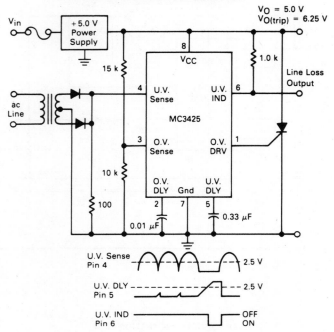

OVERVOLTAGE AUDIO ALARM CIRCUIT

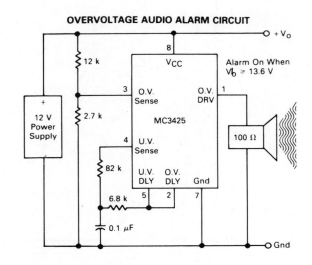

PROGRAMMABLE FREQUENCY SWITCH

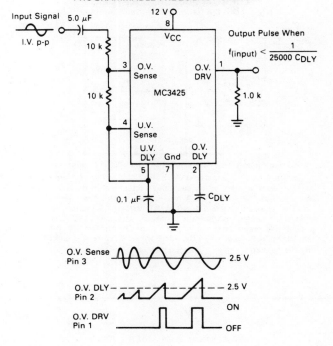

MC7905

CURRENT REGULATOR

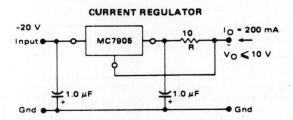

The MC7905, -5.0 V regulator can be used as a constant current source when connected as above. The output current is the sum of resistor R current and quiescent bias current as follows:

$$I_O = \frac{5.0\ V}{R} + I_B$$

The quiescent current for this regulator is typically 4.3 mA. The 5.0 volt regulator was chosen to minimize dissipation and to allow the output voltage to operate to within 6.0 V below the input voltage.

CURRENT BOOST REGULATOR
(-5.0 V @ 4.0 A, with 5.0 A current limiting)

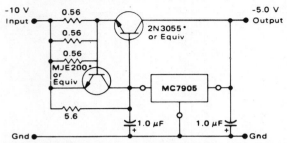

*Mounted on common heat sink, Motorola MS-10 or equivalent.

When a boost transistor is used, short-circuit currents are equal to the sum of the series pass and regulator limits, which are measured at 3.2 A and 1.8 A respectively in this case. Series pass limiting is approximately equal to 0.6 V/R_{SC}. Operation beyond this point to the peak current capability of the MC7905C is possible if the regulator is mounted on a heat sink; otherwise thermal shutdown will occur when the additional load current is picked up by the regulator.

OPERATIONAL AMPLIFIER SUPPLY
(± 15 V @ 1.0 A)

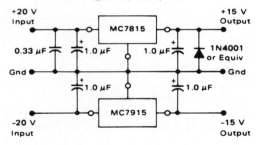

The MC7815 and MC7915 positive and negative regulators may be connected as shown to obtain a dual power supply for operational amplifiers. A clamp diode should be used at the output of the MC7815 to prevent potential latch-up problems whenever the output of the positive regulator (MC7815) is drawn below ground with an output current greater than 200 mA.

MC34060

STEP-DOWN CONVERTER WITH SOFT-START AND OUTPUT CURRENT LIMITING

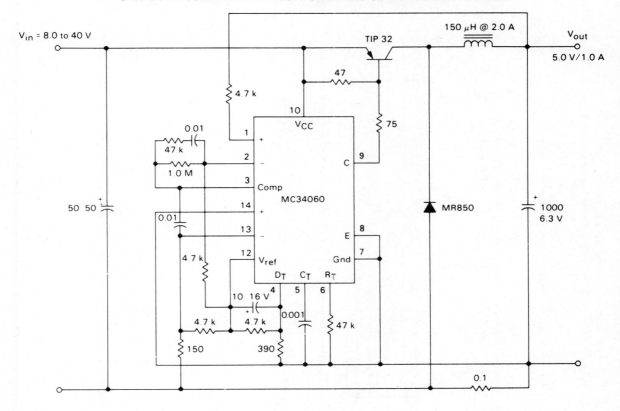

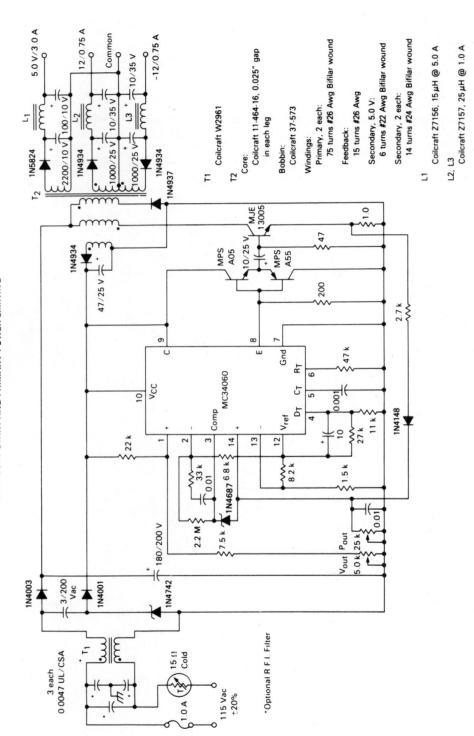

**33 WATT OFF-LINE FLYBACK CONVERTER
WITH SOFT-START AND PRIMARY POWER LIMITING**

T1   Coilcraft W2961

T2
Core: Coilcraft 11-464-16, 0.025" gap
          in each leg
Bobbin: Coilcraft 37-573
Windings:
          Primary, 2 each:
          75 turns #26 Awg Bifilar wound
          Feedback:
          15 turns #26 Awg
          Secondary, 5.0 V:
          6 turns #22 Awg Bifilar wound
          Secondary, 2 each:
          14 turns #24 Awg Bifilar wound

L1   Coilcraft 27156, 15 μH @ 5.0 A
L2, L3 Coilcraft 27157, 25 μH @ 1.0 A

*Optional R.F.I. Filter

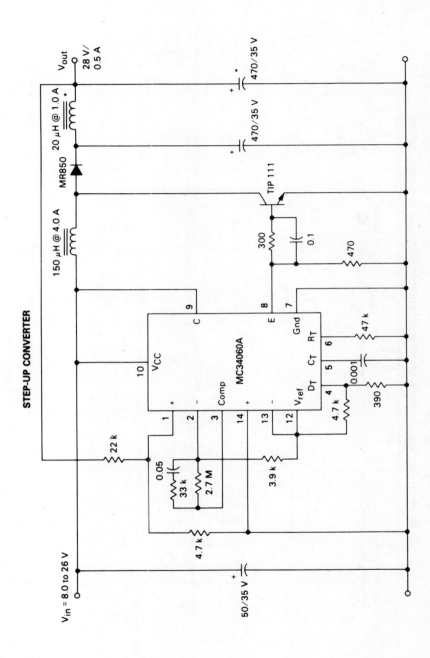

STEP-UP CONVERTER

STEP-UP/DOWN VOLTAGE INVERTING CONVERTER WITH SOFT-START AND CURRENT LIMITING

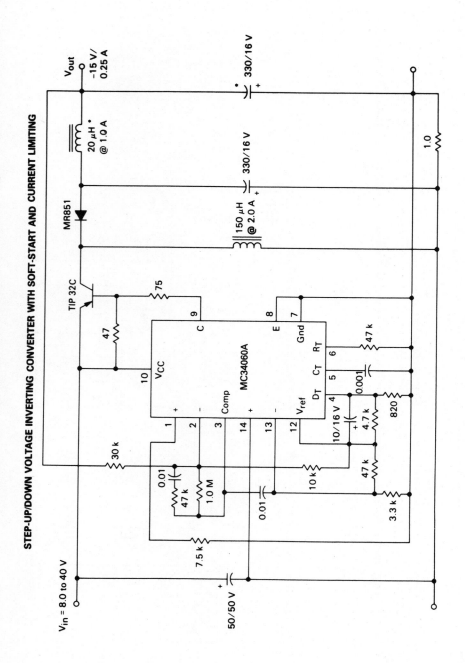

MC34064, MC33064

LOW VOLTAGE MICROPROCESSOR RESET

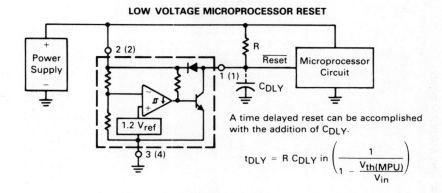

A time delayed reset can be accomplished with the addition of C_{DLY}.

$$t_{DLY} = R\,C_{DLY}\,\ln\left(\frac{1}{1 - \dfrac{V_{th(MPU)}}{V_{in}}}\right)$$

VOLTAGE MONITOR

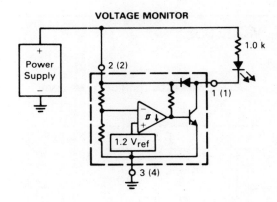

SOLAR POWERED BATTERY CHARGER

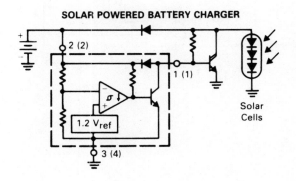

LOW POWER SWITCHING REGULATOR

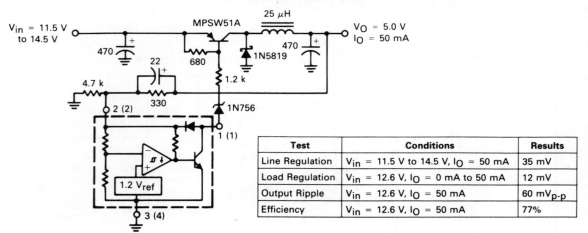

Test	Conditions	Results
Line Regulation	V_{in} = 11.5 V to 14.5 V, I_O = 50 mA	35 mV
Load Regulation	V_{in} = 12.6 V, I_O = 0 mA to 50 mA	12 mV
Output Ripple	V_{in} = 12.6 V, I_O = 50 mA	60 mV$_{p-p}$
Efficiency	V_{in} = 12.6 V, I_O = 50 mA	77%

MC34065, MC33065

ADJUSTABLE REDUCTION OF CLAMP LEVEL

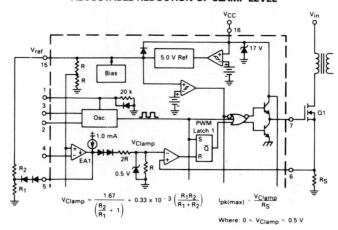

$$V_{Clamp} \approx \frac{1.67}{\left(\frac{R_2}{R_1} + 1\right)} + 0.33 \times 10^{-3} \left(\frac{R_1 R_2}{R_1 + R_2}\right) \qquad I_{pk(max)} \approx \frac{V_{Clamp}}{R_S}$$

Where: $0 \approx V_{Clamp} \approx 0.5$ V

SOFT-START CIRCUIT

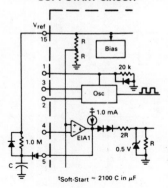

$t_{Soft\text{-}Start} \approx 2100\ C$ in μF

ADJUSTABLE REDUCTION OF CLAMP LEVEL
WITH SOFT-START

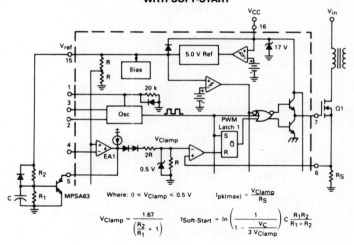

Where: $0 \leq V_{Clamp} \leq 0.5$ V

$$I_{pk(max)} \approx \frac{V_{Clamp}}{R_S}$$

$$V_{Clamp} \approx \frac{1.67}{\left(\frac{R_2}{R_1} + 1\right)}$$

$$t_{Soft\text{-}Start} = \ln\left(\frac{1}{1 - \frac{V_C}{3\ V_{Clamp}}}\right) C\ \frac{R_1 R_2}{R_1 + R_2}$$

MOSFET PARASITIC OSCILLATIONS

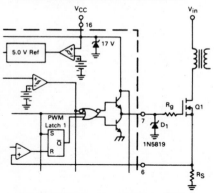

Series gate resistor R_g may be needed to damp high frequency parasitic oscillations caused by the MOSFET input capacitance and any series wiring inductance in the gate-source circuit. R_g will decrease the MOSFET switching speed. Schottky diode D_1 is required if circuit ringing drives the output pin below ground.

CURRENT SENSING POWER MOSFET

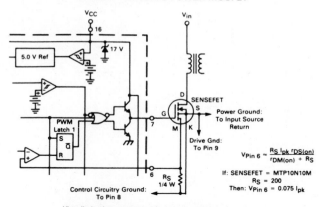

$$V_{Pin\ 6} \approx \frac{R_S\ I_{pk}\ r_{DS(on)}}{r_{DM(on)} + R_S}$$

If: SENSEFET = MTP10N10M
R_S = 200
Then: $V_{Pin\ 6}$ = 0.075 I_{pk}

Virtually lossless current sensing can be achieved with the implementation of a SENSEFET power switch. For proper operation during over current conditions, a reduction of the $I_{pk(max)}$ clamp level must be implemented. Refer to Figures 19 and 21.

CURRENT WAVEFORM SPIKE SUPPRESSION

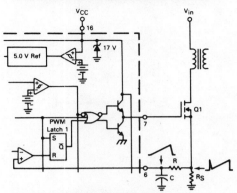

The addition of the RC filter will eliminate instability caused
by the leading edge spike on the current waveform.

DUAL CHARGE PUMP CONVERTER

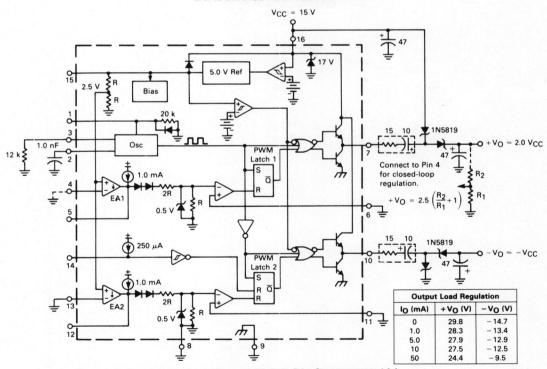

$+V_O \approx 2.0\ V_{CC}$

Connect to Pin 4
for closed-loop
regulation.

$+V_O = 2.5\left(\dfrac{R_2}{R_1}+1\right)$

$-V_O \approx -V_{CC}$

Output Load Regulation		
I_O (mA)	$+V_O$ (V)	$-V_O$ (V)
0	29.8	−14.7
1.0	28.3	−13.4
5.0	27.9	−12.9
10	27.5	−12.5
50	24.4	−9.5

The capacitor is equivalent series resistance must limit the Drive Output current to 1.0 A.
An additional series resistor may be required when using tantalum or other low ESR
capacitors. The positive output can provide excellent line and load regulation by
connecting the R2/R1 resistor divider as shown.

BIPOLAR TRANSISTOR DRIVE

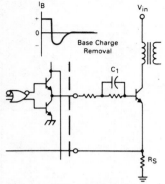

The totem-pole outputs can furnish negative base current for enhanced transistor turn-off, with the addition of capacitor C_1.

ISOLATED MOSFET DRIVE

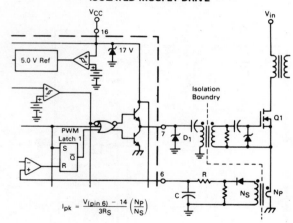

$$I_{pk} = \frac{V_{(pin\ 6)} - 14}{3R_S} \left(\frac{N_P}{N_S}\right)$$

MC34129, MC33129

**EXTERNAL DUTY CYCLE CLAMP
AND MULTI UNIT SYNCHRONIZATION**

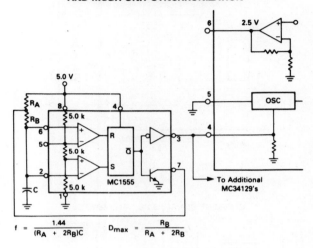

$$f = \frac{1.44}{(R_A + 2R_B)C} \qquad D_{max} = \frac{R_B}{R_A + 2R_B}$$

BOOTSTRAP START-UP

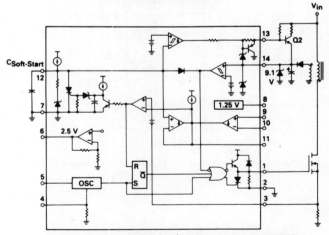

The external 9.1 V zener is required when driving low threshold MOSFETs.

267

DISCRETE STEP REDUCTION OF CLAMP LEVEL

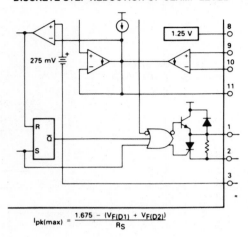

$$I_{pk(max)} = \frac{1.675 - (V_{F(D1)} + V_{F(D2)})}{R_S}$$

CURRENT SENSING POWER MOSFET

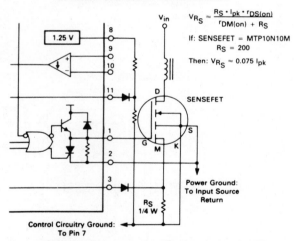

$$V_{R_S} \approx \frac{R_S \cdot I_{pk} \cdot r_{DS(on)}}{r_{DM(on)} + R_S}$$

If: SENSEFET = MTP10N10M
$R_S = 200$

Then: $V_{R_S} \approx 0.075\ I_{pk}$

Virtually lossless current sensing can be achieved with the implementation of a SENSEFET power switch.

CURRENT WAVEFORM SPIKE SUPPRESSION

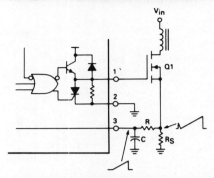

The addition of the RC filter will eliminate instability caused by the leading edge spike on the current waveform.

BIPOLAR TRANSISTOR DRIVE

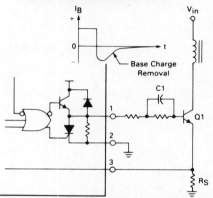

The totem-pole output can furnish negative base current for enhanced transistor turn-off, with the addition of capacitor C1.

MOSFET PARASITIC OSCILLATIONS

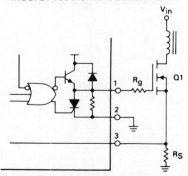

Series gate resistor R_g will damp any high frequency parasitic oscillations caused by the MOSFET input capacitance and any series wiring inductance in the gate-source circuit.

ADJUSTABLE REDUCTION OF CLAMP LEVEL

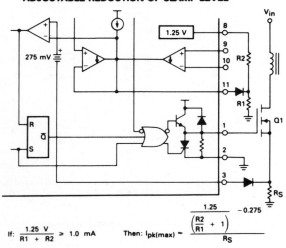

If: $\dfrac{1.25 \text{ V}}{R1 + R2} \geq 1.0 \text{ mA}$ Then: $I_{pk(max)} \approx \dfrac{\dfrac{1.25}{\left(\dfrac{R2}{R1} + 1\right)} - 0.275}{R_S}$

NON-ISOLATED 725 mW FLYBACK REGULATOR

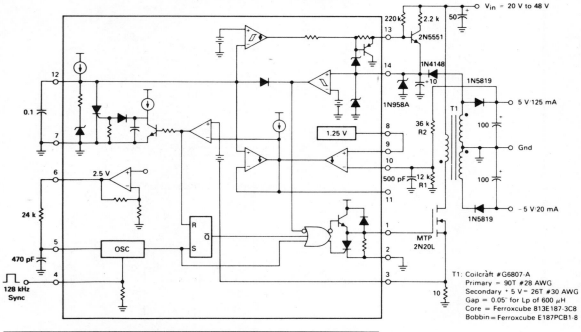

T1: Coilcraft #G6807-A
Primary = 90T #28 AWG
Secondary + 5 V = 26T #30 AWG
Gap = 0.05" for Lp of 600 μH
Core = Ferroxcube 813E187-3C8
Bobbin = Ferroxcube E187PCB1-8

Test	Conditions	Results
Line Regulation 5 V	V_{in} = 20 V to 40 V, I_{out} 5 V = 125 mA, I_{out} −5 V = 20 mA	Δ = 1.0 mV
Load Regulation 5 V	V_{in} = 30 V, I_{out} 5 V = 0 mA to 150 mA, I_{out} −5 V = 20 mA	Δ = 2.0 mV
Output Ripple 5 V	V_{in} = 30 V, I_{out} 5 V = 125 mA, I_{out} −5 V = 20 mA	150 mVp-p
Efficiency	V_{in} = 30 V, I_{out} 5 V = 125 mA, I_{out} −5 V = 20 mA	77%

$$V_{out} = 1.25 \left(\frac{R2}{R1} + 1\right)$$

270

MC34160, MC33160

TYPICAL MICROPROCESSOR APPLICATION

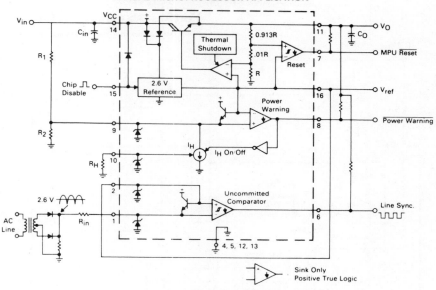

LINE LOSS DETECTOR APPLICATION

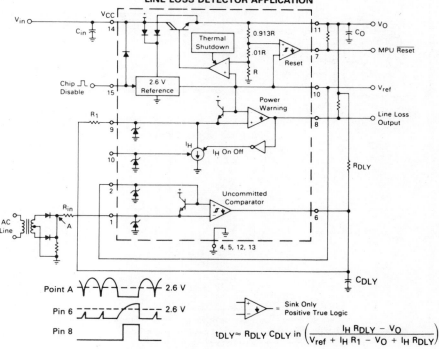

$$t_{DLY} \approx R_{DLY}\, C_{DLY} \, \text{ln}\left(\frac{I_H\, R_{DLY} - V_O}{V_{ref} + I_H\, R_1 - V_O + I_H\, R_{DLY}}\right)$$

SG1525A

LAB TEST FIXTURE

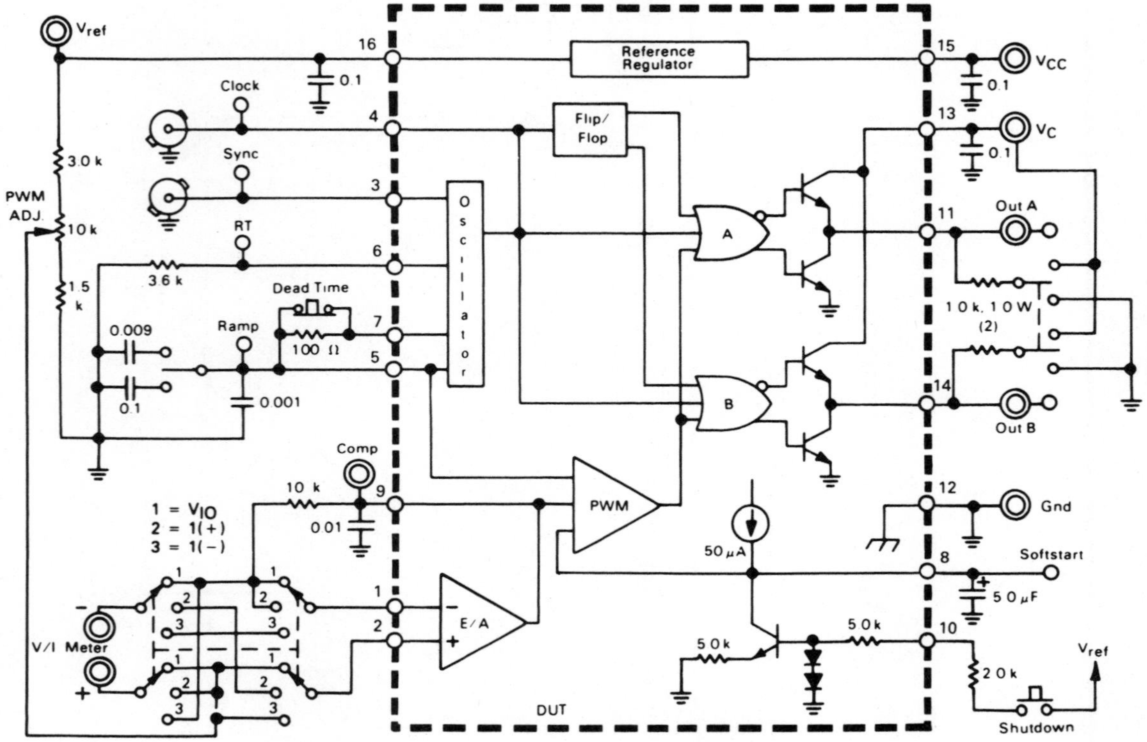

SINGLE ENDED SUPPLY

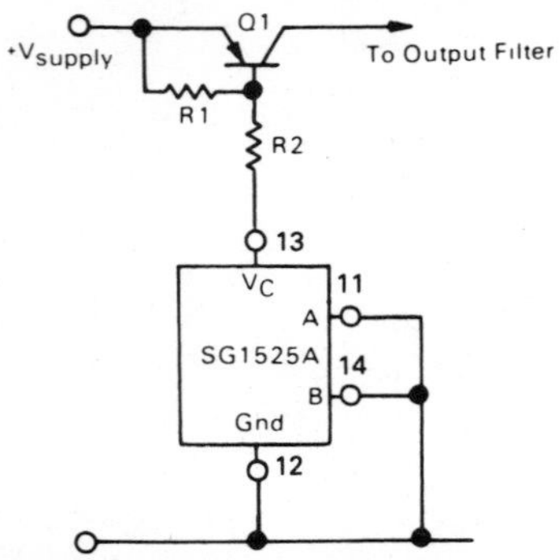

For single-ended supplies, the driver outputs are grounded. The V_C terminal is switched to ground by the totem-pole source transistors on alternate oscillator cycles.

272

PUSH-PULL CONFIGURATION

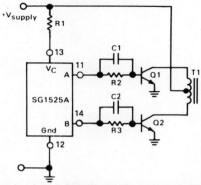

In conventional push-pull bipolar designs, forward base drive is controlled by R1–R3. Rapid turn-off times for the power devices are achieved with speed-up capacitors C1 and C2.

DRIVING TRANSFORMERS IN A HALF-BRIDGE CONFIGURATION

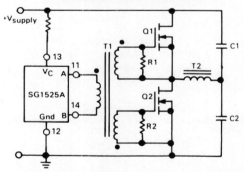

Low power transformers can be driven directly by the SG1525A. Automatic reset occurs during deadtime, when both ends of the primary winding are switched to ground.

273

DRIVING POWER FETS

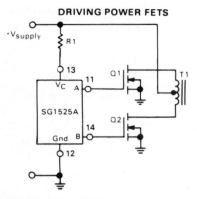

The low source impedance of the output drivers provides rapid charging of power FET input capacitance while minimizing external components.

SG1526, SG2526, SG3526

**EXTENDING REFERENCE
OUTPUT CURRENT CAPABILITY**

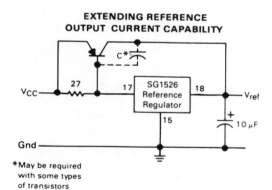

*May be required
with some types
of transistors

ERROR AMPLIFIER CONNECTIONS

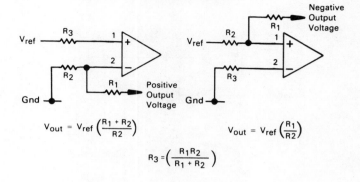

$$V_{out} = V_{ref} \left(\frac{R_1 + R_2}{R_2} \right)$$

$$V_{out} = V_{ref} \left(\frac{R_1}{R_2} \right)$$

$$R_3 = \left(\frac{R_1 R_2}{R_1 + R_2} \right)$$

OSCILLATOR CONNECTIONS

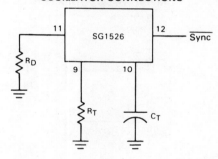

FOLDBACK CURRENT LIMITING

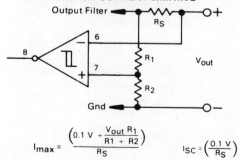

$$I_{max} = \frac{\left(0.1 \text{ V} + \frac{V_{out} R_1}{R_1 + R_2} \right)}{R_S} \qquad I_{SC} = \left(\frac{0.1 \text{ V}}{R_S} \right)$$

SG1526 SOFT-START CIRCUITRY

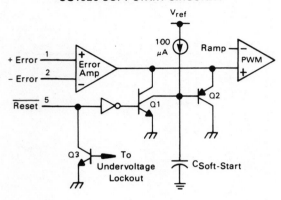

DRIVING VMOS POWER FETS

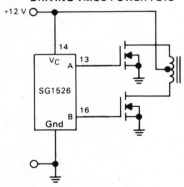

The totem pole output drivers of the SG1526 are ideally suited for driving the input capacitance of power FETs at high speeds.

PUSH-PULL CONFIGURATION

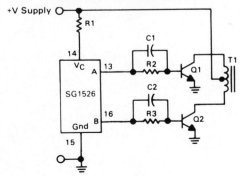

HALF-BRIDGE CONFIGURATION

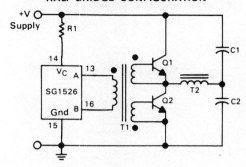

FLYBACK CONVERTER WITH CURRENT LIMITING

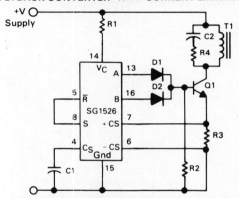

In the above circuit, current limiting is accomplished by using the current limit comparator output to reset the soft-start capacitor.

SINGLE-ENDED CONFIGURATION

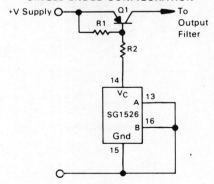

ADUSTABLE REDUCTION OF CLAMP LEVEL

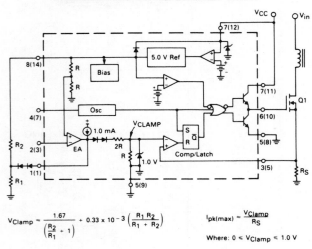

$$V_{Clamp} \approx \frac{1.67}{\left(\frac{R_2}{R_1} + 1\right)} + 0.33 \times 10^{-3} \left(\frac{R_1 \, R_2}{R_1 + R_2}\right)$$

$$I_{pk(max)} \approx \frac{V_{Clamp}}{R_S}$$

Where: $0 \leq V_{Clamp} \leq 1.0 \text{ V}$

ADJUSTABLE BUFFERED REDUCTION OF
CLAMP LEVEL WITH SOFT-START

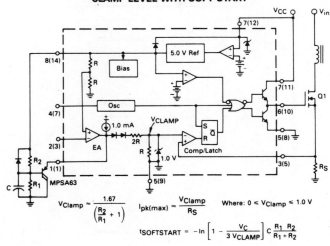

$$V_{Clamp} \approx \frac{1.67}{\left(\frac{R_2}{R_1} + 1\right)}$$

$$I_{pk(max)} \approx \frac{V_{Clamp}}{R_S}$$

Where: $0 \leq V_{Clamp} \leq 1.0 \text{ V}$

$$t_{SOFTSTART} = -\ln\left[1 - \frac{V_C}{3 \, V_{CLAMP}}\right] C \frac{R_1 \, R_2}{R_1 + R_2}$$

EXTERNAL CLOCK SYNCHRONIZATION

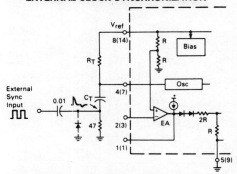

The diode clamp is required if the Sync amplitude is large enough to cause the bottom side of C_T to go more than 300 mV below ground.

SOFT-START CIRCUIT

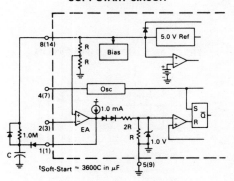

$t_{Soft-Start} \approx 3600C$ in μF

EXTERNAL DUTY CYCLE CLAMP AND
MULTI UNIT SYNCHRONIZATION

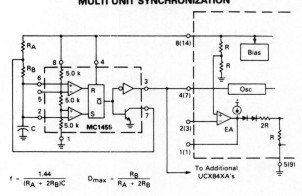

$$f = \frac{1.44}{(R_A + 2R_B)C} \qquad D_{max} = \frac{R_B}{R_A + 2R_B}$$

279

CURRENT SENSING POWER MOSFET

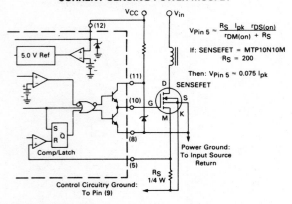

$$V_{Pin\ 5} \approx \frac{R_S\ I_{pk}\ r_{DS(on)}}{r_{DM(on)} + R_S}$$

If: SENSEFET = MTP10N10M
$$R_S = 200$$

Then: $V_{Pin\ 5} \approx 0.075\ I_{pk}$

Virtually lossless current sensing can be achieved with the implementation of a SENSEFET power switch. For proper operation during over current conditions, a reduction of the $I_{pk(max)}$ clamp level must be implemented. Refer to Figures 22 and 24.

ERROR AMPLIFIER COMPENSATION

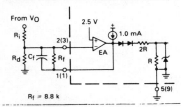

Error Amp compensation circuit for stabilizing any current-mode topology except for boost and flyback converters operating with continuous inductor current.

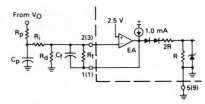

Error Amp compensation circuit for stabilizing current-mode boost and flyback topologies operating with continuous inductor current.

CURRENT WAVEFORM SPIKE SUPPRESSION

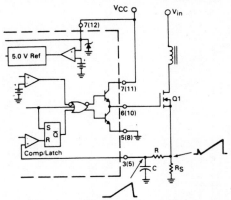

The addition of the RC filter will eliminate instability caused by the leading edge spike on the current waveform.

MOSFET PARASITIC OSCILLATIONS

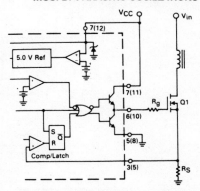

Series gate resistor R_g will damp any high frequency parasitic oscillations caused by the MOSFET input capacitance and any series wiring inductance in the gate-source circuit.

ISOLATED MOSFET DRIVE

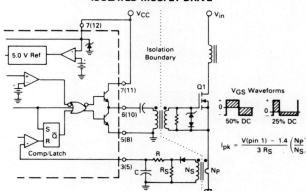

$$I_{pk} = \frac{V(\text{pin 1}) - 1.4}{3\,R_S}\left(\frac{N_P}{N_S}\right)$$

BIPOLAR TRANSISTOR DRIVE

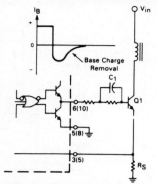

The totem-pole output can furnish negative base current for enhanced transistor turn-off, with the addition of capacitor C_1.

LATCHED SHUTDOWN

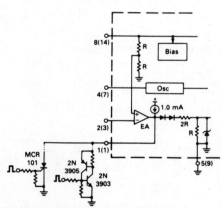

The MCR101 SCR must be selected for a holding of less than 0.5 mA at $T_{A(min)}$. The simple two transistor circuit can be used in place of the SCR as shown. All resistors are 10 k.

VOLTAGE REGULATORS *(RAY)*

4191/2/3 (Micro-Power Switching Regulators)

9.0V Battery Life Extender

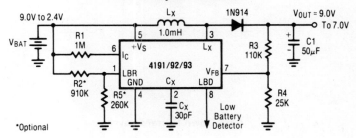

Bootstrapped Operation

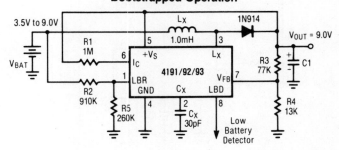

9.0V Battery Life Extender

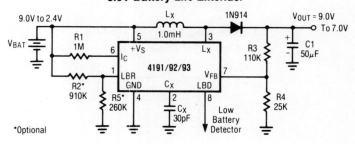

Complete Step-Down Regulator

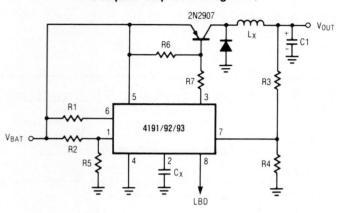

Step-Down Current Saver

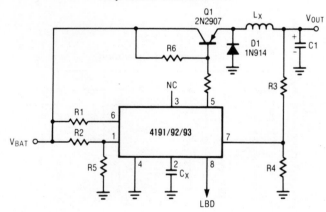

Simple Step-Down DC-to-DC
Converter ($V_O \le V_{BAT}$)

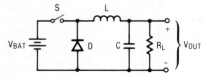

Step-Up Switching Regulator (High Current)

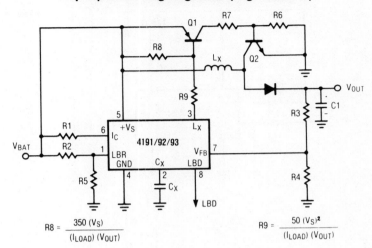

$$R8 = \frac{350\ (V_S)}{(I_{LOAD})\ (V_{OUT})}$$

$$R9 = \frac{50\ (V_S)^2}{(I_{LOAD})\ (V_{OUT})}$$

Stepping Down an Input Voltage Greater Than 30V (High Current)

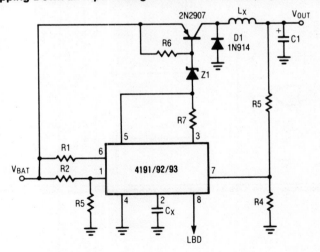

Stepping Down an Input Voltage Greater Than 30V

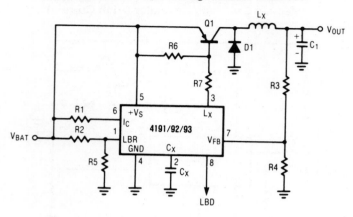

Battery Back-Up Circuit

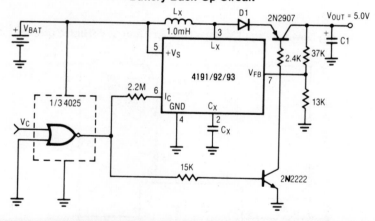

8

Switches and Multiplexers

All circuits in this chapter are courtesy of Silconix.

DG201A/202

Precision Instrumentation Amplifier with Digitally Programmable Gains

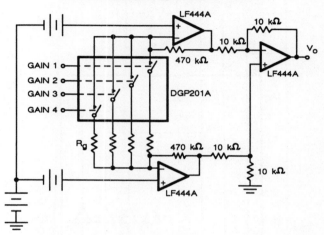

Sample-and-Hold Circuit

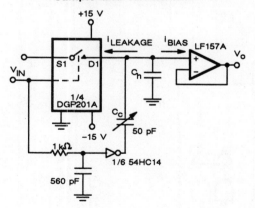

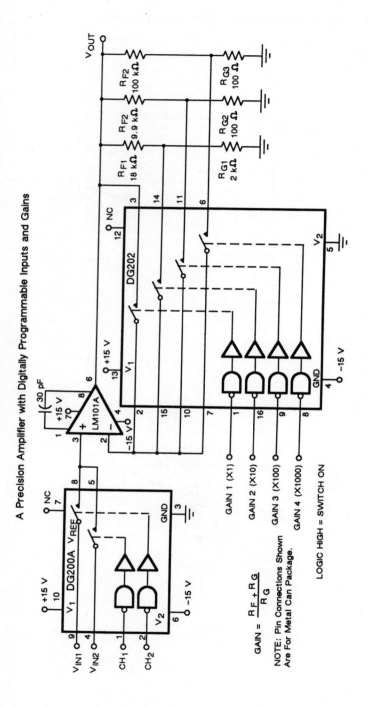

A Precision Amplifier with Digitally Programmable Inputs and Gains

$$GAIN = \frac{R_F + R_G}{R_G}$$

NOTE: Pin Connections Shown Are For Metal Can Package.

LOGIC HIGH = SWITCH ON

DG211/212

Microprocessor Controlled Analog Signal Attenuator

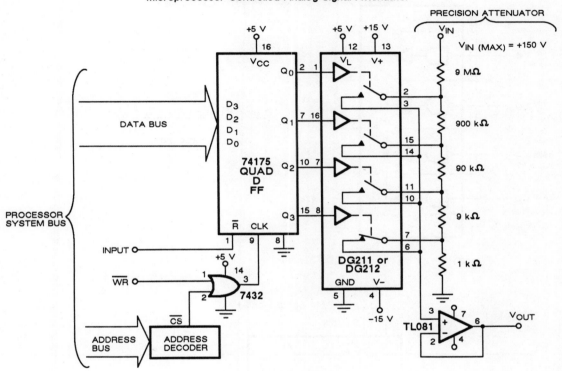

Four-Channel Analog Multiplexer

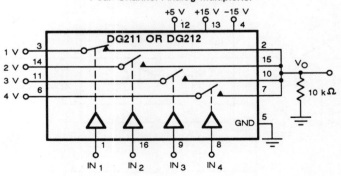

Precision-Weighted Resistor Programmable-Gain Amplifier

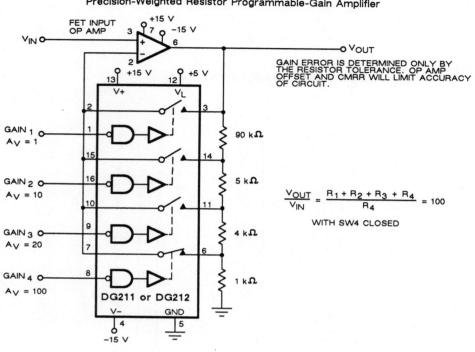

GAIN ERROR IS DETERMINED ONLY BY THE RESISTOR TOLERANCE. OP AMP OFFSET AND CMRR WILL LIMIT ACCURACY OF CIRCUIT.

$$\frac{V_{OUT}}{V_{IN}} = \frac{R_1 + R_2 + R_3 + R_4}{R_4} = 100$$

WITH SW4 CLOSED

DG211 Sample-and-Hold

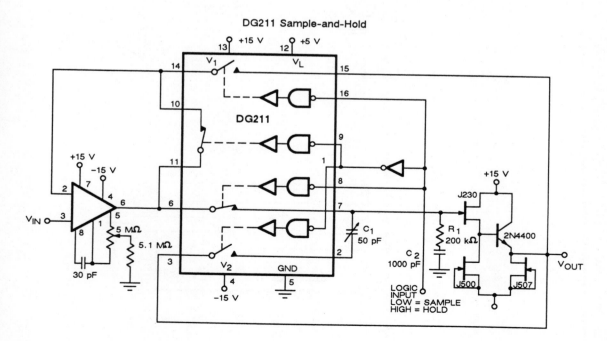

μP Controlled Analog Signal Attenuator

The TL081 is used as unity gain buffer while DG221
selected voltage divider provides attenuation.

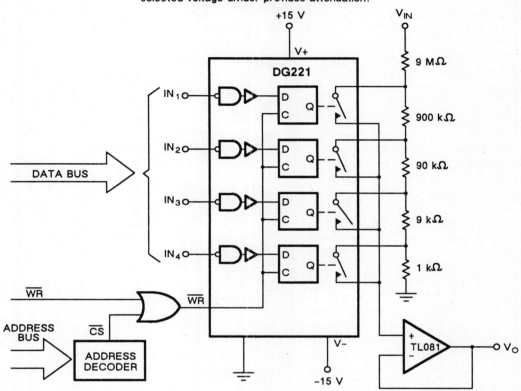

**Low Power Instrumentation Amplifier with
Digitally Selectable Inputs and Gain**

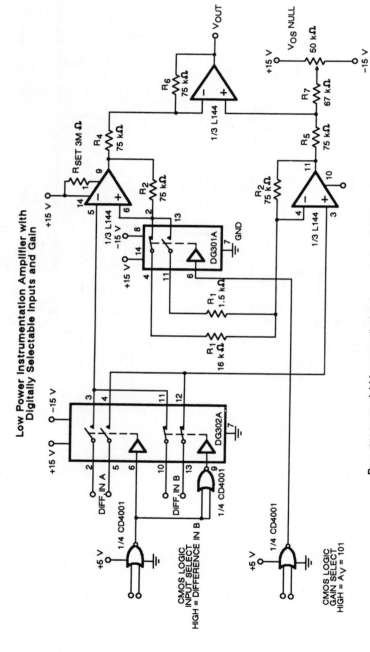

R_{SET} programs L144 power dissipation, gain–bandwidth product.
Refer to AN73-6 and the L144 data sheet.

Voltage gain of the Instrumentation amplifier is :

$$A_V = 1 + \frac{2R_2}{R_1}$$ (In the circuit shown, $A_{V1} = 10.4$, $A_{V2} = 101$)

DG304A/305A/306A/307A

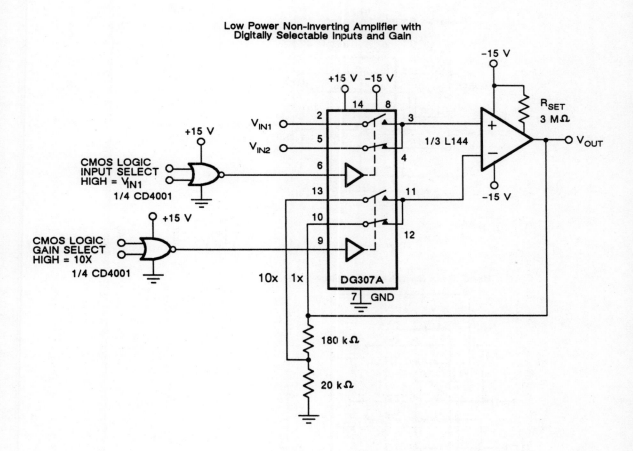

Low Power Non-Inverting Amplifier with
Digitally Selectable Inputs and Gain

DG403

Stereo Source Selector

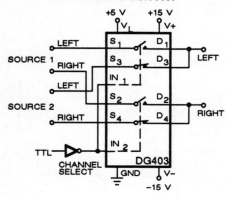

Band-Pass Switched Capacitor Filter

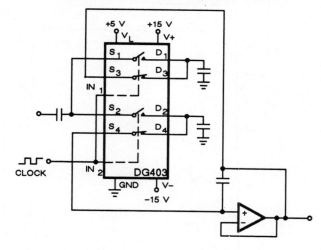

Dual Slope Integrator

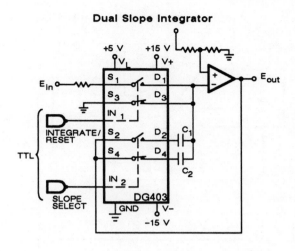

Summing Amplifier

12-Bit Plus Sign Magnitude D/A Converter

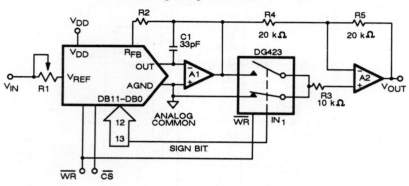

12-Bit Plus Sign Magitude Code Table

SIGN BIT	DIGITAL INPUT MSB LSB	ANALOG OUTPUT (V_{OUT})
0	1111 1111 1111	$+(4095/4096)V_{IN}$
0	0000 0000 0000	0 VOLTS
1	0000 0000 0000	0 VOLTS
1	1111 1111 1111	$+(4095/4096)V_{IN}$

DG444/445

Precision-Weighted Resistor Programmable-Gain Amplifier

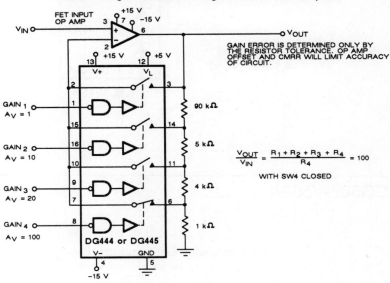

GAIN ERROR IS DETERMINED ONLY BY THE RESISTOR TOLERANCE. OP AMP OFFSET AND CMRR WILL LIMIT ACCURACY OF CIRCUIT.

$$\frac{V_{OUT}}{V_{IN}} = \frac{R_1 + R_2 + R_3 + R_4}{R_4} = 100$$

WITH SW4 CLOSED

Precision Sample-and-Hold

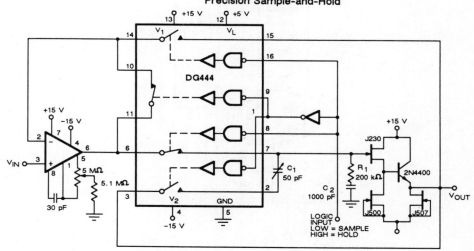

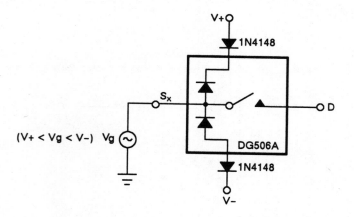

DG508A/509A

8 Channel Sequential Mux/Demux

Overvoltage Protection Using Blocking Diodes

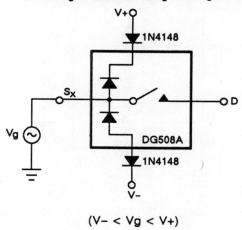

$$(V- < V_g < V+)$$

Differential 4 Channel Sequential Mux/Demux

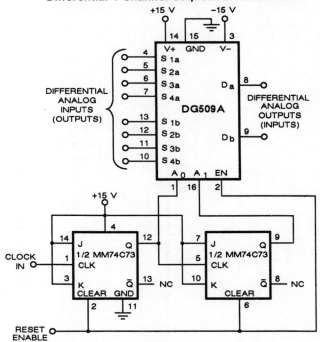

High Performance Video Switch

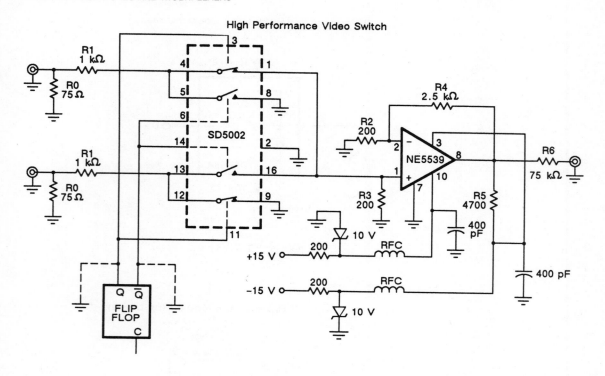

Driver for MOSPOWER H-Switch

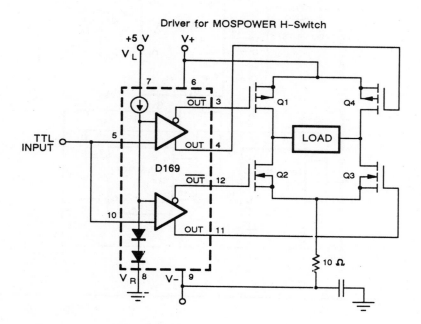

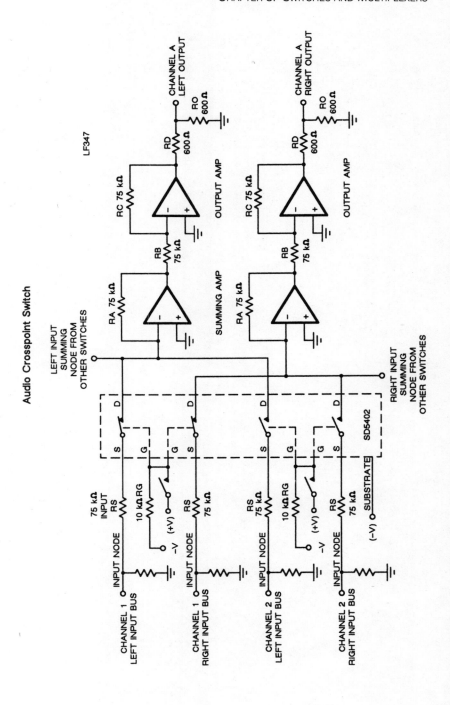

Audio Crosspoint Switch

9

Voltage References
and
V-F Converters

VOLTAGE REFERENCES *(MO)*

SHUNT REGULATOR

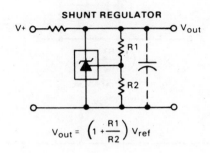

$$V_{out} = \left(1 + \frac{R1}{R2}\right) V_{ref}$$

HIGH CURRENT SHUNT REGULATOR

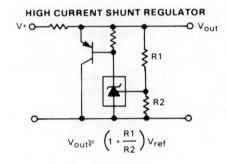

$$V_{out} = \left(1 + \frac{R1}{R2}\right) V_{ref}$$

OUTPUT CONTROL OF A
THREE-TERMINAL FIXED REGULATOR

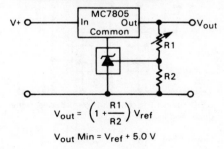

$$V_{out} = \left(1 + \frac{R1}{R2}\right) V_{ref}$$

$$V_{out} \text{ Min} = V_{ref} + 5.0 \text{ V}$$

SERIES PASS REGULATOR

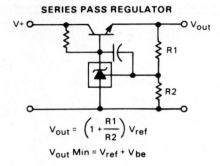

$$V_{out} = \left(1 + \frac{R1}{R2}\right) V_{ref}$$

$$V_{out} \text{ Min} = V_{ref} + V_{be}$$

TL431,A Series

CONSTANT CURRENT SOURCE

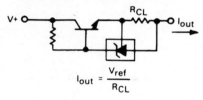

$$I_{out} = \frac{V_{ref}}{R_{CL}}$$

VOLTAGE MONITOR

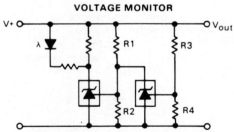

L.E.D. indicator is 'on' when V+ is between the upper and lower limits.

$$\text{Lower Limit} = \left(1 + \frac{R1}{R2}\right) V_{ref}$$

$$\text{Upper Limit} = \left(1 + \frac{R3}{R4}\right) V_{ref}$$

CONSTANT CURRENT SINK

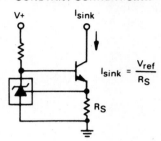

$$I_{sink} = \frac{V_{ref}}{R_S}$$

TRIAC CROWBAR

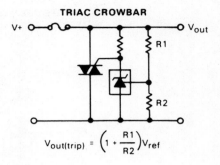

$$V_{out(trip)} = \left(1 + \frac{R1}{R2}\right)V_{ref}$$

SCR CROWBAR

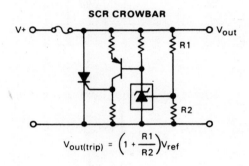

$$V_{out(trip)} = \left(1 + \frac{R1}{R2}\right)V_{ref}$$

LINEAR OHMMETER

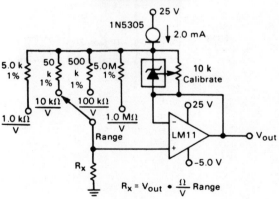

$$R_x = V_{out} \bullet \frac{\Omega}{V} \ Range$$

SINGLE-SUPPLY COMPARATOR WITH
TEMPERATURE-COMPENSATED THRESHOLD

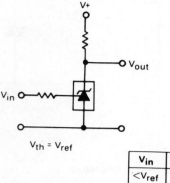

$V_{th} = V_{ref}$

V_{in}	V_{out}
$<V_{ref}$	V+
$>V_{ref}$	≈ 2.0 V

SIMPLE 400 mW PHONO AMPLIFIER

$T_I = 330\ \Omega$ to $8.0\ \Omega$

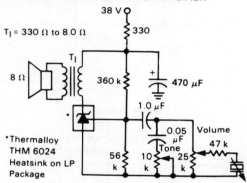

*Thermalloy
THM 6024
Heatsink on LP
Package

MC1408 Series/MC1508

**COMBINED OUTPUT AMPLIFIER and
VOLTAGE REFERENCE CIRCUIT**

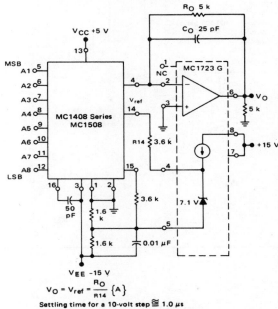

$$V_O = V_{ref} = \frac{R_O}{R14} \{A\}$$

Settling time for a 10-volt step $\cong$ 1.0 μs

**BIPOLAR OR INVERTED NEGATIVE
OUTPUT VOLTAGE CIRCUIT**

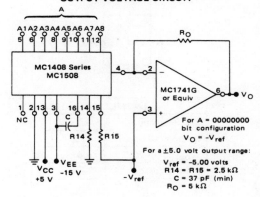

For A = 00000000
bit configuration
$V_O = -V_{ref}$

For a ±5.0 volt output range:
V_{ref} = –5.00 volts
R14 = R15 = 2.5 kΩ
C = 37 pF (min)
R_O = 5 kΩ

Decrease R_O to 2.5 kΩ for a 0 to –5.0-volt output range.
This application provides somewhat lower speed, as previously
discussed in the Output Voltage Range section of the General
Information.

BIPOLAR OR NEGATIVE OUTPUT
VOLTAGE CIRCUIT

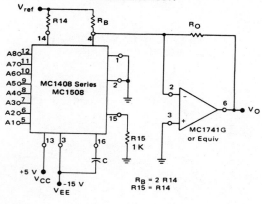

$$V_O = \frac{V_{ref}}{R14}(R_O)\left[\frac{A1}{2} + \frac{A2}{4} + \frac{A3}{8} + \frac{A4}{16} + \frac{A5}{32} + \frac{A6}{64} + \frac{A7}{128} + \frac{A8}{256}\right] - \frac{V_{ref}}{R_B}(R_O)$$

MC10319

V_{RT} VOLTAGE SOURCE

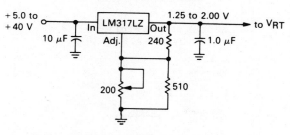

LM317LZ	
Line Regulation	1.0 mV
T_C (ppm/°C) max	60
ΔV_{out} for 0–70°C	8.4 mV
Initial Accuracy	±4%

PRECISION V_{RT} VOLTAGE SOURCE

R1 = 100 Ω for +5.0 V
620 Ω for +15 V

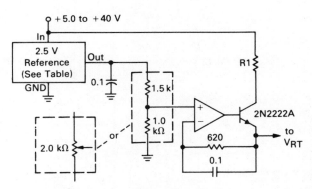

2.5 V References	MC1400G2	MC1403U	MC1403AU
Line Regulation	1.0 mV	0.5 mV	0.5 mV
T_C (ppm/°C) max	25	40	25
ΔV_{out} for 0–70°C	4.4 mV	7.0 mV	4.4 mV
Initial Accuracy	± 0.2%	± 1%	± 1%

V_{RB} VOLTAGE SOURCES

R1 = 100 Ω for −5.0 V
620 Ω for −15 V
R2 = 620 Ω for −5.0 V
3.0 kΩ for −15 V

	MC1400G2	LM337MT
Line Regulation	1.0 mV	1.0 mV
T_C (ppm/°C) max	25	48
ΔV_{out} for 0–70°C	4.4 mV	6.7 mV
Initial Accuracy	± 0.2%	± 4%

313

1Hz→100MHz Voltage-to-Frequency Converter (King Kong V→F) (LT)

+15V +5.2V

LT317A

121Ω

390Ω

CURRENT SINK
+7.5V
1000M

+7.5V

LT317A

121Ω

619Ω

−5V

−15V LT337A

121Ω

360Ω

8.2k

43k   30k

16k

1k

BUFFER   TRIGGER

+7.5V

A3
EL2004

82Ω

12
13

+5.2V

9
15

2k

−5V

¼ MC10H102
4pF

220

RAMP RESET

2N3904

12k   120Ω

200k

MV209
5pF–40pF

1μF

ECL ÷16

+5.2V

CK   MC10136 ÷16

S1   CARRY IN

390

390

¼ MC10H102

+15V

390   620

2N5160

620

−5V

¼ MC10H102

LEVEL SHIFT

+5.2V

D   Q̄
CK CD4013
Q

−5V   −5V

÷2 CHARGE
PUMP DRIVE

OUTPUT
1Hz–100MHz

SERVO AMP

0.1   0.1

−5V

A1
LTC1052

C_COMP

(SEE TEXT)

5k**

10k

A2
½LT1013

VARACTOR BIAS AMP

INPUT
0V–10V

2k
100MHz
TRIM

CHARGE PUMP

0.22

+5.2V

−5V

390

LTC1043

4   17   16

LT1009
2.5V

−5V   220

8   7

11

100pF†

12

14   13

6   5

2

3

100pF†

18   15

100*

+5.2V

50k

200

10k
1Hz
TRIM

10M

200

50k

−5V

1μF

EL2004 = ELANTEC
†POLYSTYRENE
*1% FILM RESISTOR
**TRW MTR-5/ +120ppm/°C

10k

10k

A4
½LT1013

LINEARITY BIAS AMP

50k
LINEARITY
TRIM

1Hz → 2.5MHz Fast Response V → F (LT)

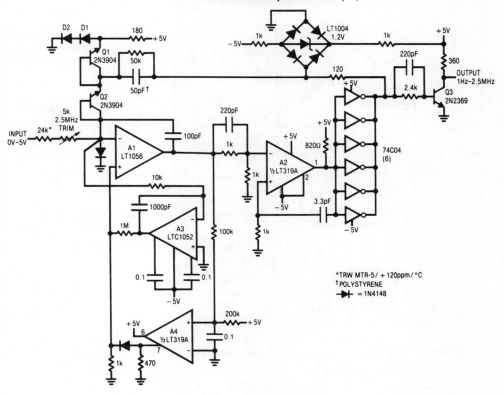

D169 Used as a Voltage-to-Frequency Converter (SIL)

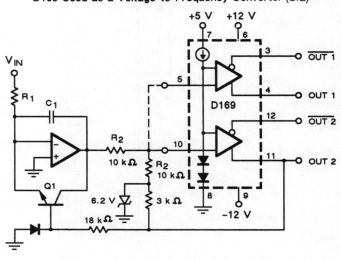

Quartz-Stabilized V → F (LT)

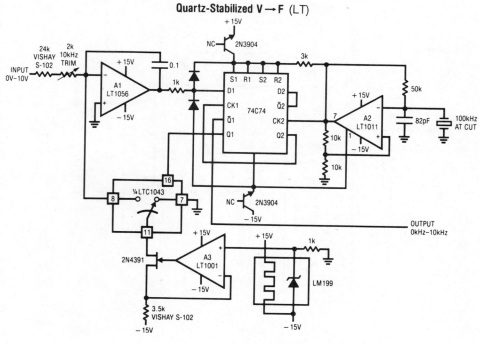

Ultra-Linear V → F (LT)

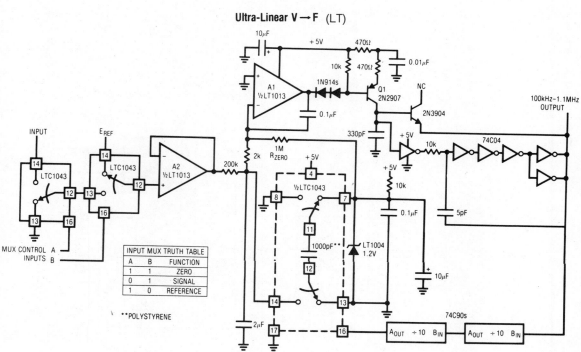

INPUT MUX TRUTH TABLE		
A	B	FUNCTION
1	1	ZERO
0	1	SIGNAL
1	0	REFERENCE

**POLYSTYRENE

Single Cell V → F (LT)

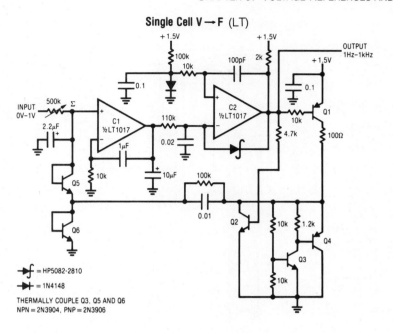

Sine Wave Output 1Hz → 100kHz V → F (VCO) (LT)

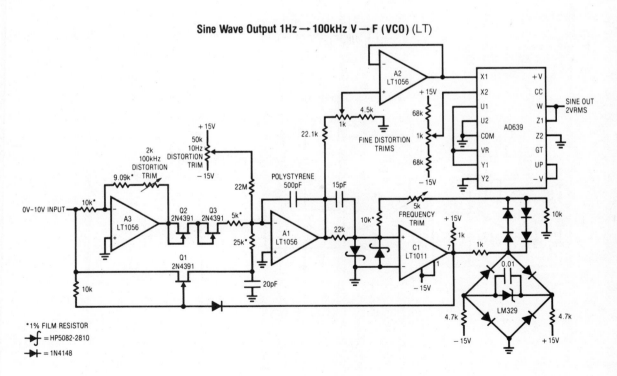

$E_{IN}{}^X \rightarrow$ Frequency Converter (LT)

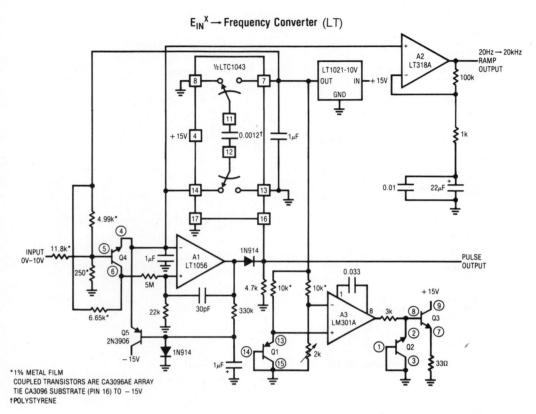

*1% METAL FILM
 COUPLED TRANSISTORS ARE CA3096AE ARRAY
 TIE CA3096 SUBSTRATE (PIN 16) TO −15V
†POLYSTYRENE

$\dfrac{I}{E_{IN}} \rightarrow$ Frequency Converter (LT)

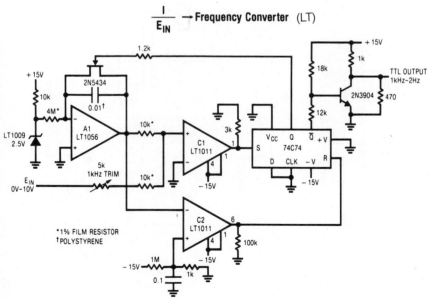

*1% FILM RESISTOR
†POLYSTYRENE

$$\frac{R1}{R2} = \frac{V1}{V2} \longrightarrow \textbf{Frequency Converter} \text{ (LT)}$$

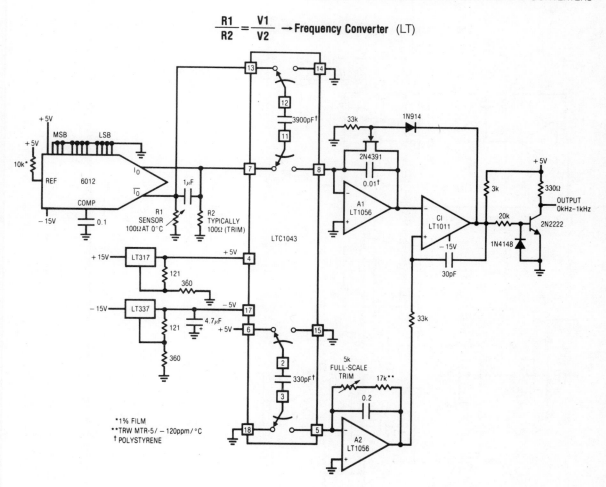

Charge Pump $\dfrac{1}{E_{IN}}$ → Frequency Converter (LT)

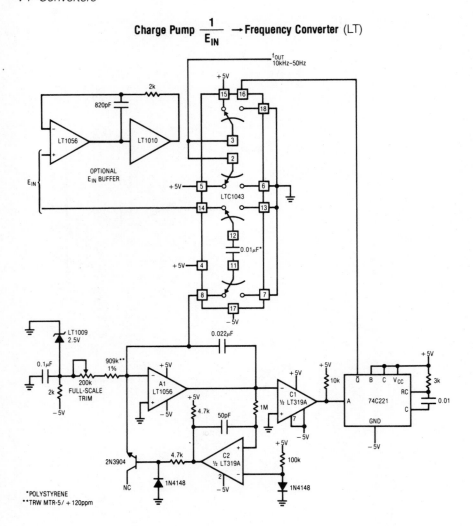

Index

Components Index

Other Bestsellers of Related Interest

PROGRAMMABLE CONTROLLERS: Hardware, Software, and Applications—George L. Batten, Jr., Ph.D.

This book provides process engineers and technicans with a ready source of basic information on using programmable controllers to achieve a wide variety of manufacturing goals. You'll find flowcharts and step-by-step explanations of how programmable controllers can be used to develop more more efficient process control . . . save labor through increased automation . . . improve product quality . . . and monitor complicated procedures from a remote location. 304 pages, 187 illustrations. Book No. 3147, $32.95 hardcover only

HIGH-POWER ELECTRONICS—W. James Sarjeant and R.E. Dollinger

This is the first real reference to the field of high-power electronics written in the last 25 years. The authors have compiled this timely guide from a series of lectures given by themselves and other professionals. Designed as a working benchtop reference, the major focus of this book is on system design and pulse components in high-repetition-rate systems for powering such devices as gas discharge lasers, accelerators, free electron lasers, and radar. 416 pages, 336 illustration. Book No. 3094, $42.95 hardcover only

INTERNATIONAL ENCYCLOPEDIA OF INTEGRATED CIRCUITS—Stan Gibilisco

How would you like to have the answers to just about any IC or IC application question in one easy-to-use ''master'' source? Now you can, with the new, all-inclusive *International Encyclopedia of Integrated Circuits*. This convenient quick-reference source provides pin-out diagrams, internal block diagrams and schematics, characteristic curves, descriptions and applications—for foreign and domestic ICs! 1,000 pages, 4,500 illustrations. Book No. 3100, $69.50 hardcover only

New in the Computer Graphics Technology and Management Series . . .
AutoCAD PROGRAMMING—Dennis N. Jump

CAD expert Dennis Jump offers you a straightfoward, comprehensive guide to the popular CAD software package that includes version 2.0. Jump explains in detail the data structures and algorithms associated with AutoCAD programming, including numerous sample program listings in both C and BASIC. You'll learn how to write application programs that use AutoCAD as a companion, as well as how to use data within AutoCAD to display the images, drawings, diagrams, and more created with your application programs. 288 pages, 150 illustrations. Book No. 3093, $24.95 paperback, $39.95 hardcover